COOKING
SOUS VIDE

RICHER FLAVORS • BOLDER COLORS • BETTER NUTRITION

ALPHA

Publisher: Mike Sanders
Associate Publisher: Billy Fields
Senior Acquisitions Editor: Brook Farling
Development Editor: Kayla Dugger
Cover and Book Designer: Rebecca Batchelor
Photographer: Daniel Showalter
Food Stylist: Allison Douglass
Recipe Tester: Geoff Kelty
Prepress Technician: Ayanna Lacey
Proofreader: Amy Borrelli
Indexer: Celia McCoy

First American Edition, 2016
Published in the United States by DK Publishing
6081 E. 82nd Street, Indianapolis, Indiana 46250

Copyright © 2016 Dorling Kindersley Limited

A Penguin Random House Company

16 17 18 19   10 9 8 7 6 5 4 3 2 1

001–295094–October/2016

Published in the United States by Dorling Kindersley Limited.

IDIOT'S GUIDES and Design are trademarks of Penguin
Random House LLC

ISBN: 978-1-4654-5349-5

Library of Congress Catalog Card Number: 2016935495

Note: This publication contains the opinions and ideas of its
author. It is intended to provide helpful and informative
material on the subject matter covered. It is sold with the
understanding that the author and publisher are not engaged in
rendering professional services in the book. If the reader
requires personal assistance or advice, a competent
professional should be consulted.

DK books are available at special discounts when purchased in
bulk for sales promotions, premiums, fund-raising, or
educational use. For details, contact:
DK Publishing Special Markets, 345 Hudson Street,
New York, New York 10014
or SpecialSales@dk.com.

Printed and bound in the United States

idiotsguides.com

COOKING
SOUS VIDE

RICHER FLAVORS • BOLDER COLORS • BETTER NUTRITION

Chef Thomas N. England

contents

Introduction to Sous Vide

WHAT IS
SOUS vide?

Sous vide is a French term that translates to "under vacuum." The sous vide process involves sealing food in a bag and cooking it in a temperature-controlled water bath.

Cooking "Under Vacuum"

Originally referring to the process of vacuum sealing food in order to extend its shelf life, sous vide became known as a cooking process in the 1940s. At that time, people began experimenting with placing vacuum-sealed food in a pot of boiling water to heat it.

This rudimentary process wasn't refined until the 1970s, when a European scientist tested water temperatures in relation to sealed packages of food being cooked. His discoveries led to the adoption of sous vide as a tool to cook gourmet foods.

However, it really wasn't until 2000 that chefs in the United States started to understand and utilize the technique. By then, immersion circulators could heat water to exact temperatures. Thus, sous vide cooking became much more controlled and attainable.

How Sous Vide Is Different

Unlike traditional methods of cooking, sous vide cooks food evenly and at a lower temperature, leading to a better finished product.

Normally, foods are placed onto a heat source that's much hotter than the ideal temperature of the final cooked food. For instance, a piece of filet mignon is often sautéed at a temperature between 300°F and 500°F (149°C and 260°C); however, the desired internal temperature is 135°F (57°C) for medium-rare steak. This results in a piece of meat that varies from very well done near the outside to medium-rare in the middle. With sous vide cooking, the filet mignon can be seasoned, put into a bag, and cooked in a water bath set to exactly 135°F (57°C). In just a few minutes, the whole steak is exactly medium-rare; it can then be put in a very hot sauté pan for a few seconds to gain a flavorful brown exterior.

The sous vide technique also sets itself apart when it comes to cooking tougher cuts of meat. Normally, tough cuts are braised at a high temperature in order for the connective tissue to melt. For instance, a tough meat may be braised in a flavorful liquid in a 250°F (121°C) oven for 3 hours. If it's cooked at too hot of a temperature though, the moisture literally boils out of the meat. With sous vide, the seasoned meat can be sealed in a plastic bag and placed in a water bath set at a much lower temperature. Because connective tissue readily melts at 150°F (66°C), you get a juicier slice of meat than if you braised it.

What sets sous vide apart from other methods is its ability to evenly cook any food.

Why Cook Sous Vide?

Beyond cooking foods evenly and at the perfect temperature, sous vide helps seal in flavor and nutrition. For instance, when making soup, you're likely familiar with how the smells of the broth waft through the air. While this helps build the feeling of hunger, it also means the smells in the air are no longer in the soup. Sous vide makes up for the loss of those delicious smells by sealing them into the bag, resulting in food that truly bursts with a multitude of flavors.

When it comes to nutrition, you can use sous vide to preserve the nutrients in your food, as it takes into account the different temperatures at which food still maintains them. So you don't have to rely on outdated cooking methods that can rob foods of nutrients. Instead, you can cook your food at the ideal temperature and end up with foods that yield the best nutrition, because the nutrients aren't lost to less efficient cooking methods. For instance, you can cook green beans sous vide at just the right temperature so the bright green colors develop and the chlorophylls release their nutrients.

Based on these benefits, it's easy to see why sous vide cooking is becoming popular in homes everywhere.

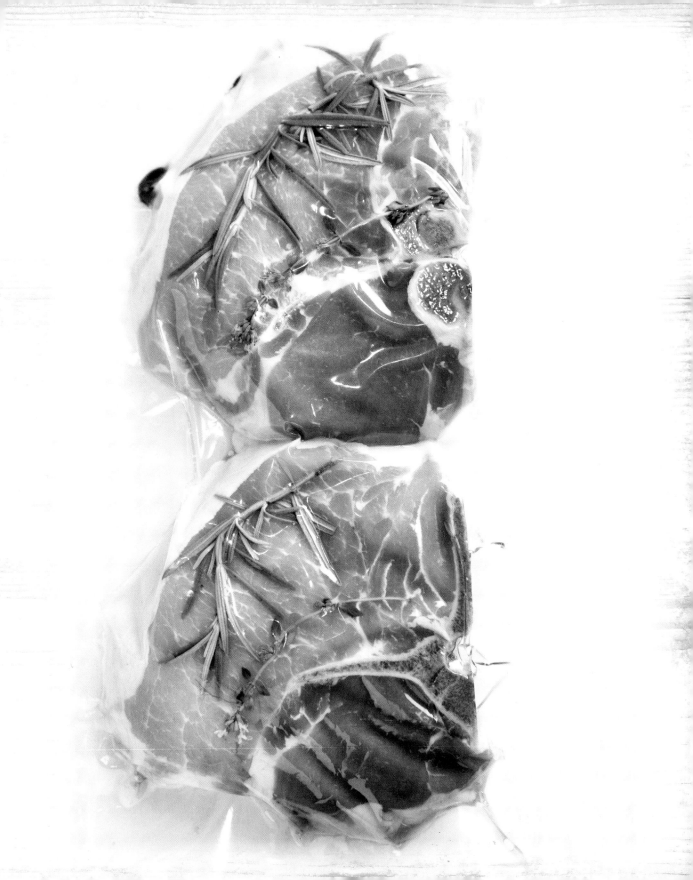

HOW DOES SOUS VIDE **work?**

The sous vide process differs from traditional cooking by using water instead of air to transfer heat, allowing you to set more precise cook times and letting you cook to an exact temperature. This method results in food that's perfectly cooked.

Without Oxygen

Oxygen is the enemy of freshness. When heating up foods using convential cooking methods, the food molecules expand and allow oxygen to enter as they heat up (a process known as *oxidation*). Oxidation causes foods to lose their flavor and color. On the other hand, sous vide packaging removes oxygen from the equation by requiring you to seal foods in plastic bags or jars. This prevents oxidation, keeping your foods bright and flavorful.

When cooking food in a conventional oven, moisture and aromas can be leached out due to the type of open-air vessel being used, such as a baking pan, a casserole dish, and so on. By sealing foods in plastic bags or jars, you lock in the pleasant aromas and water vapor, so you end up with cooked foods that are moist and full of flavor.

Wrapped salmon

Unwrapped salmon

More Precise Times

While cooking times for sous vide are usually longer than for conventional methods, the longer times are more forgiving, meaning you're less likely to overcook food and more likely to achieve the results you desire. For instance, tough cuts of meat are typically cooked at higher temperatures over a shorter period of time to break down the connective tissue and make them tender, which tends to dry them out. When you cook these cuts sous vide at lower temperatures over a longer time frame, however, the connective tissues are still broken down without a loss in moisture.

Steak cooked sous vide for 20 minutes at 145°F (63°C)

Steak cooked sous vide for 2 hours at 145°F (63°C)

More Exact Temperatures

Traditional cooking methods require you to set temperatures much higher than the food actually needs; this is done to ensure the center is cooked and to kill off any bacteria. With sous vide, you can accomplish the same thing without sacrificing taste. The machine is simply set at the required temperature necessary for doneness, so you get a product cooked to your liking that's also safe to eat.

These eggs were cooked for the same amount of time, with the egg on the left at a temperature slightly lower than the egg on the right

145°F (63°C)

150°F (66°C)

SOUS VIDE
machines

When it comes to cooking food sous vide, keeping the water at an exact temperature is crucial. Maintaining consistent heat during the process is primarily accomplished by a water oven or an immersion circulator.

While both sous vide machines are capable of maintaining temperature, they vary in terms of cost, range of temperatures, and calibration guarantee. In terms of cost, water ovens range from $400 to $1,400. On the other hand, immersion circulators are a bit more affordable, with a starting price of $100, though high-end versions can cost thousands of dollars.

When evaluating machines, you should also look at the temperature ranges they can maintain for long periods of time. The temperatures should range from 126°F to 190°F (52°C to 88°C). Some devices may have difficulty maintaining low temperatures and will cycle too hot.

A third consideration when choosing a machine is the guarantee of calibration. When cooking sous vide, a variation of 1 degree can make a big difference. Look for a guarantee with a variation of only a ½ degree.

Water Oven

A water oven is an insulated container with a heating element surrounding the inside of a water bath chamber. The temperature of the oven is controlled by a preset temperature you input through controls on the outside of the appliance. Additionally, there may be a heating element under the container to raise the temperature more quickly as needed.

A water oven has a lid that seals in the heat. This helps maintain a consistent temperature within the oven without any loss of heat energy.

Because there's no pump in a sous vide water oven, you can pour and heat liquids–such as stocks and other infusions–directly into the chamber without having to use plastic bags.

Some water ovens come with a vacuum sealer and plastic bags as part of a package deal. This is ideal if you are just getting started and have yet to purchase those supplies on your own.

Immersion Circulator

An immersion circulator combines a pump, heater, and thermometer all in one device. The circulator pumps water up from the bottom of a container, heats it to an exact temperature, and recirculates it through the container. The pump continuously runs in order to regulate the heat, which helps keep the water at a constant temperature.

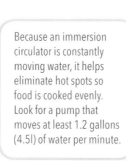

An immersion circulator gives you more flexibility, as the machine can be placed in any container. So unlike a water oven, what you decide to cook sous vide isn't limited by the size of the water chamber.

Because an immersion circulator is constantly moving water, it helps eliminate hot spots so food is cooked evenly. Look for a pump that moves at least 1.2 gallons (4.5l) of water per minute.

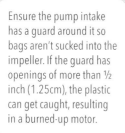

Ensure the pump intake has a guard around it so bags aren't sucked into the impeller. If the guard has openings of more than ½ inch (1.25cm), the plastic can get caught, resulting in a burned-up motor.

Professional Machines

Professional circulators and large combi ovens were the only choice for sous vide cooking until the advent of cheaper home versions. Professional immersion circulators typically set themselves apart from the home versions due to speed. Whereas most home versions will pump water at about 1.2 gallons (4.5l) per minute, professional versions can go as high as 3.2 gallons (12.1l) per minute. The main reason for the need for speed is that restaurants may have many different bags in the container at one time, meaning water needs to flow faster to get around all of the bags.

Combi ovens differ from typical sous vide water ovens because they use steam instead of a true water bath. In combi ovens, temperature-controlled water vapor is blown across the sous vide packages. This allows for a constant flow of water in an exact temperature across a very large oven, so hundreds of sous vide bags can be cooked at one time.

While this professional gear is great for the controlled cooking of many items, it isn't really needed by most home cooks.

SOUS VIDE
basics

The sous vide process includes four basic steps: prep, seal, cook, and finish. Before going through each in more detail later in this part, I'd like to take you through just how all of them work together to create a delicious final product.

Cooking with Ease

While at first glance the sous vide method might appear more complex than traditional cooking methods, it's really not that complicated. You simply seal ingredients in a plastic bag, place the bag in a water bath, and hold a target temperature to within a degree or two. With your water oven or immersion circulator, you can warm a water bath to any temperature you set and keep it there for hours—or even days, if needed. When the food reaches your target temperature, you take it out, give it a quick sear or other finish, and serve it. That's it.

For softer foods that might get squished during the vacuum-sealing process (such as ground beef), you have the option of using a zipper-lock bag instead.

Sous Vide: Not Just for Steak

Sous vide is best illustrated with steak, as that's where you'll see the most dramatic difference between how it cooks traditionally versus the sous vide way. However, you can employ the sous vide process on just about any type of food. Fruits, vegetables, poultry, pork, seafood, and even desserts all benefit from cooking sous vide.

With fruits and vegetables, you'll notice how they retain their vibrant colors when vacuum sealed due to the lack of oxygen. As for poultry, you can cook it to a safe temperature without sacrificing flavor. Leaner cuts of pork benefit because the lack of fat is made up for by keeping the moisture contained in the sealed package. Sous vide helps seafood keep its delicate, tender nature without overcooking it. And when it comes to desserts, you'll get a lighter and softer texture.

1 PREP

The first step in the cooking process includes cleaning, trimming, and adding flavors to the food. These flavorings could be in the form of seasonings, herbs, rubs, or marinades.

2 SEAL

Most often, the second step is done using a heavy-duty plastic bag that's sealed using a vacuum sealer. This type of packaging removes air from around the food, allowing for a more even cooking surface when placed in a water bath.

When you cut into a food cooked sous vide, you'll notice how evenly it's cooked, as well as how much moisture it has retained

3 COOK

The third step is completed in a water oven or using an immersion circulator. The wrapped food floats in a water bath and cooks to the desired temperature, retaining moisture and flavor usually lost with other methods.

4 FINISH

With this final step, you remove the food from the plastic and get it ready to serve. This could involve anything from chilling it in the refrigerator, to boiling it with other ingredients (such as when making a soup), to searing the exterior to caramelize it.

You can **finish a piece of meat** by searing it in a sauté pan, on a grill, or with a blowtorch.

prep

Whether it's removing seafood shells or peeling vegetables, your food needs some prep work before being sealed in a bag. Fortunately, preparing food for sous vide is as easy as cooking it.

While prep work for sous vide is slightly different than for traditional cooking, it's not a completely foreign concept. Meat and poultry are still dried and crustaceans are still shelled the same way they are with conventional methods.

However, certain preparation steps involve adding something to the bag to ensure the food retains its natural appearance—such as oil to reduce albumen on seafood, or vinegar to enrich the color of certain vegetables.

You'll also notice that any food that contains sharp bones or shells—such as poultry or seafood—requires the removal of those bones and shells before sealing and cooking. Otherwise, the bones or shells could break through the bags and ruin the food. So take special care to prep your ingredients, and enjoy the first step in the sous vide process.

Meat

Remove excess fat

Form ground meat into a ball

- Trim away any excess fat.
- Dry meats to allow seasoning to stick to the protein.
- Arrange meats in the shape you want them to be when finally cooked so they're easier to place in sous vide bags.

Poultry

- Dry poultry with a paper towel. This lowers foodborne illness risks when you slide poultry into the plastic bags, as the meat is likely to touch the exterior of the bags.
- To make the meat juicier, you may cure poultry during this time.
- When it comes to a dish like coq au vin, sear poultry as part of the preparation process.

Debone chicken

In some cases, you may need to debone chicken. This is done not only to ensure the bones aren't consumed, but also to keep the bones from penetrating the plastic bag during cooking.

Seafood

- Seafood lends itself well to brining before cooking. Simply brine the seafood for 1 hour before seasoning and packaging.

- As with poultry, debone fish and remove shrimp and lobster shells so the shells and bones don't penetrate the plastic bags.

- Adding oil to seafood beforehand helps reduce the unsightly white albumen that forms on the outside as it's cooked and maintains the fish's shape during sealing.

Remove the shells using a pair of kitchen scissors

Vegetables

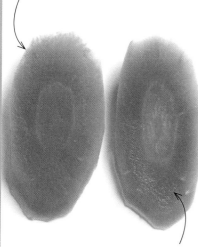

Firmness and moisture are lost when peeled before cooking

Peeling after cooking helps retain firmness and moisture

- Thoroughly wash vegetables to remove any dirt before cooking. This ensures that foodborne illnesses aren't grown during the cooking process.

- Avoid peeling vegetables as part of prep. Otherwsie, ridges and raised dots will form as the cell structure falls apart and loses moisture. Cooked vegetables are easier to cut and peel and have cleaner appearance.

- For white root vegetables, add a bit of oil to the bag with them to help them retain their color.

- For red and purple vegetables, add vinegar to the bag to enrich their color.

PREPPING ALCOHOL FOR SOUS VIDE COOKING

Typically used in marinades or sauces, alcohol is an important part of cooking. However, there are certain issues you should be aware of when prepping it for use during the sous vide process.

Because alcohol will start to steam at 160°F (71°C), you must heat the liquor before putting it in the bag. Otherwise, it will create an air space as it cooks, which could cause the bag to break open or lead to your food being unevenly cooked. Also, because alcohol doesn't boil off when cooked sous vide, it can lend a harsh, unpleasant taste to your food.

To prepare alcohol for sous vide cooking, simply boil it with the other marinade or sauce ingredients until it's reduced by half. Once reduced, pour the liquid into a container and allow it to chill in the refrigerator for a few minutes. You can then add the liquid to the plastic sous vide bag with your food before placing the bag in the machine.

Seasoning

Seasoning is an essential component of sous vide preparation. Anything from a simple sprinkling of salt and pepper to marinating imparts flavor to food that's then further enhanced through the sous vide process.

BEFORE OR AFTER?

There's been a big debate in the sous vide world concerning how much you should season foods during prep versus after the bag comes out of the water.

Some purists believe the magic of sous vide is how the cooking process brings out the natural flavors of the food, which could be compromised by mixing other flavors in with the bag beforehand. The other side of the debate—and the philosophy I follow in this book—is that seasonings and other flavors will have more impact if they are sealed in with the food and allowed to penetrate during the cooking process.

However, one process isn't better than the other. Feel free to experiment and develop your own philosophy. No matter what, you'll always have a great meal.

SALTING

Salt is the most highly discussed topic when it comes to sous vide cooking. With conventional cooking techniques, salts are applied to the exterior of meats to help with the browning process. By putting kosher or sea salt on the outside of meat before sautéing, grilling, or broiling, the salt will soak up water on the exterior of the meat. This allows heat to get directly to the meat and caramelize it. However, because high heat isn't in direct contact with meat during sous vide cooking, you really don't need the caramelization qualities in salt before cooking.

Salt also has an osmotic effect, transferring the calcium into the protein cell and thereby releasing some of the water from the cell in the process. This effect can cause the meat to lose some of its moisture and tighten up, making it firmer and drier. In most cases, you don't want this osmotic effect. Therefore, if you're cooking meat sous vide for an extended amount of time, you shouldn't add salt to it beforehand. However, if you're cooking the meat more quickly (less than 2 hours from seasoning to service), you can add salt from the start.

In most cases, adding salt after the cooking process is the best practice. Dry the meat with a paper towel after it's removed from the package, and then add the kosher or sea salt. You can then sear, grill, or use a blowtorch to get the carmelization you desire for your meat.

BRINING

Brining is when you enhance the flavor of a food and create a firmer product by soaking it in a salt solution. However, because brining may actually cause a drop in the moisture levels of some foods, it's generally discouraged. If you're working with a food that's usually brined, such as seafood, ham, or pickles, you can follow these steps when cooking sous vide.

1 At a rate of 1 tablespoon salt per 1 quart (1l) water, combine water, salt, and any spices to make a brining liquid.

2 While keeping below 70°F (21°C), place the brining liquid and the food together in a plastic zipper-lock bag. Seal the bag, removing as much air as possible.

3 After brining for the specified time based on thickness, remove the food from the bag and rinse under cold running water, making sure to remove all the brine from the exterior.

MARINATING

Marinating is the process of adding flavor to food by letting it sit in a liquid comprised of acidics, spices, and occasionally oils. You should only use a marinade before cooking sous vide if the food will be completely cooked and served within 20 hours. Otherwise, the acids will continue to break down the proteins, causing the food to turn to a soft consistency.

1 Combine marinade ingredients in a blender or large bowl until they're fully dissolved.

2 While keeping the marinade below 70°F (21°C), place the marinade and the food together in a plastic zipper-lock bag. Seal the bag, removing as much air as possible.

3 After cooking it sous vide, remove the food from the bag and rinse under cold running water, making sure to remove all the marinade from the exterior.

AROMATICS

Aromatics are vegetables and herbs that infuse their aromas into the food being cooked. Adding a bit of oil to the bag before adding the aromatics will help keep the aromatics from sticking to the food.

COMMON AROMATICS

Garlic: A pungent aromatic with a spicy, bitter flavor in its raw form, it adds to a mellow, sweeter taste to food when cooked

Bay leaf: Adds a subtle citrus flavor to food

Thyme: Provides a distinctive flavor commonly associated with soup broth

Onion: Depending on the type, can give food a sweet or spicy flavor, as well as a strong aroma

Curry powder

Cinnamon

Cumin

Smoked paprika

SPICES

Spices can add a deep, earthy tone to food. They should be toasted before being added to a food that will be cooked sous vide in order to encourage the oils to come to the surface.

COMMON SPICES

Smoked paprika: Adds a smoky quality, as well as a rich, spicy tone

Curry powder: Brings a balance of lightness and boldness that makes it perfect for sous vide foods

Cumin: Commonly used with barbecue as the backbone of a rub, it has a nutty, peppery taste

Cinnamon: Brings a bright, nutty character; however, should be added sparingly to avoid overpowering the dish

Garlic

Thyme

Bay leaf

Green onion

seal

Sealing ingredients in packages is an important part of sous vide cooking. Not only does it keep out the water from the water bath, it also keeps air out of the cooking process in order to promote optimum temperature control.

There are two primary ways of packaging food before putting it into the sous vide water bath to cook. The most common way to seal sous vide packaging is to use a vacuum sealer. Once the food and seasonings are put into a precut 1-quart (1l) or 1-gallon (3.75l) plastic bag or a manually measured plastic bag from a roll, the machine pumps the air out of the bag and seals it.

The second way food can be sealed for sous vide is through the use of a zipper-lock bag. This option is great for short cooking times and doesn't require any fancy equipment. The air in the bag can be removed using the displacement method, which involves submerging the bottom of a partially sealed bag into a water bath and slowly pushing it down until the remaining air is out of the bag, at which point the bag can be sealed.

Sealing with a Vacuum Sealer

Tools needed

Vacuum sealer

Plastic bag

1 Place food in a single layer in the plastic bag, along with any liquids. (You have the option of freezing the liquids to help avoid pumping any out of the package.)

2 Clean the inside and outside lip of the plastic bag to ensure a good seal.

3 Place the open side of the plastic bag into the machine and lock it down. Adjust to seal a moist or dry food and start the machine.

Use sous vide bags that are **BPA chemical free.** That way, you'll avoid leaking dangerous toxins into the food, which can happen when plastic is exposed to heat for long periods of time.

Sealing with a Zipper-Lock Bag

Tools needed

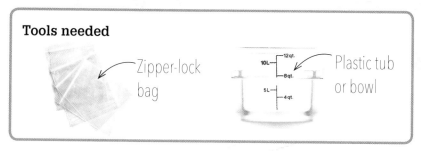

Zipper-lock bag

Plastic tub or bowl

Placing the food in the water helps seal the bag around it

1 Place food in a single layer in the zipper-lock bag, along with any liquids. (You have the option of freezing the liquids to help avoid pumping any out of the package.)

2 Seal all but a corner of the bag. Place in the water bath just up to the open corner. Once in the water, seal the rest of the way.

3 Using a clamp-style paper clip, fold the sealed edge of the zipper-lock bag over the side of the water bath container.

cook

Now that you've prepared and sealed the food, it's time to get cooking. Like a slow cooker, a sous vide machine allows you to set it and (mostly) forget it. The difference from other methods is the precise level of control you have over the cooked food.

Cooking sous vide is a matter of controlling the temperature of water around a food as it's cooking. While the circulator will control the temperature, there are a few things you'll need to monitor during the entire sous vide cooking process.

First, you need to ensure the food is surrounded by hot water at all times. If the food isn't covered completely, any part that's floating above the water won't cook. This can potentially lead to the food being in a temperature "danger zone," in which harmful bacteria can breed.

Second, you must maintain the temperature of the water during the entire cooking process. If the water isn't at the right temperature due to cold air cooling or water loss from the container, your food may get undercooked or not turn out at the doneness level you desire.

Choosing a Container to Use with an Immersion Circulator

If you plan to use an immersion circulator instead of a water oven, you may be wondering what type of container you can use to hold your water bath. While you can invest in specialized containers with lids that have cutouts to fit around the circulator, you can just as easily use a container you may already have at home.

For instance, many people use a large pot or a plastic cooler. You don't even need a lid for them, and for coolers in particular, the insulated walls help keep the water at the right temperature. One way you can maintain the water temperature without a lid is by adding a bunch of old ping-pong balls to the water bath. These not only act as double-walled insulation, they also allow you to reach through them to put in or take out the bag.

Keep an eye on **plastic bags containing vegetables,** which tend to float due to gases expelled during cooking. If this happens, remove and dry the vegetables, transfer them to a new bag, and seal. You can then add the new bag to the water.

1 **HEAT THE WATER.**
Bring the water bath up to the desired temperature using the controls on your water oven or immersion circulator. To save time, start with hot water to bring the bath up to temperature more quickly.

2 **SUBMERGE THE BAG.**
Place the plastic bag of food in the heated water bath. You can even duct tape a weight to the corner of the plastic bag to ensure it doesn't float.

3 MONITOR THE WATER TEMPERATURE.
Issues can crop up during the cook time, including plastic getting caught in the pump, the container leaking, the water level dropping below the pump, or a drop in temperature. Checking the temperature occasionally can help you spot such things.

4 REMOVE THE BAG.
Once the food has finished cooking, remove the plastic bag from the water bath by hand or with tongs.

finish

After the food has been cooked in the sous vide water bath, you can then move on to finishing the food. One aspect of finishing is browning, which is done by searing, torching, or grilling the food.

Cooking in a vacuum-sealed bag inhibits the development of umami, a pleasantly savory taste that enhances all of the other flavors in food. Searing, torching, or grilling can help you achieve this desired taste.

Browning proteins helps caramelize the meat in order to develop that umami taste. In vegetables, these methods are used to brown the natural sugars in the food. When the browning process is complete, you'll notice an obvious increase in the overall flavor of the food; the richness of the foods will pop out and make your mouth salivate.

The keys to the development of umami vary based on the process with which you choose to finish the food.

Searing

Searing is a process in which food is sautéed in a very hot pan for a short amount of time. This isn't meant to cook the middle of the food; instead, searing helps brown the exterior of the proteins, leaving them darkened and delicious.

1 Remove the food from the plastic bag and place on paper towels. Strain the liquid from the bag through a fine-mesh sieve and reserve.

2 Dry the food completely with paper towels. Once dry, season with kosher salt and then coat in vegetable oil.

3 Preheat a heavy skillet until it starts to smoke. Place the food in the skillet and allow to cook for 30 seconds on each side. Remove the food from heat.

4 Turn off the heat to the burner. Pour the reserved liquid into the still-warm skillet to heat it up. Serve as a sauce with the food.

Torching

While people typically don't turn to a torch to finish their food in home kitchens, it's often done in commercial kitchens. With the high heat produced by a torch, you can brown the outside of food without overcooking the inside.

1 Remove the food from the plastic bag and dry it completely with paper towels. Once dry, season with kosher salt.

2 Place the food on a heat-resistant plate. Sear all sides of the food by passing the blue part of the flame directly across it.

Grilling

Grilling develops extra flavor through the rapid burning of fats as they drip from the food. This flavor can be brought on in a matter of seconds after the food is cooked sous vide. Once the food is covered in oil, it can start taking on flavor the minute it hits the grate.

1 Remove the food from the plastic bag and dry it completely with paper towels. Once dry, lightly oil all sides with vegetable oil.

2 Preheat a grill to the hottest point it will go. Place the food on the hot grill and allow to cook for 30 seconds to 1 minute on each side, or until the food browns.

TOOLS

For **searing,** you need a good cast-iron skillet. Cast iron holds heat well and can be heated to high temperatures. This helps food brown quickly, which reduces moisture loss.

For **torching,** you can choose from multiple types of blowtorches. The most common is a torch that connects to a normal propane cylinder. An attachment (such as a Searzall) can be added to the tip of the blowtorch to spread out the heat for more even browning.

For **grilling,** you can use a gas or charcoal grill. However, charcoal grills tend to preheat to the required temperature much faster than gas grills. The surface of the grill should be able to reach temperatures above 600°F (316°C).

Developing Texture & Flavor

Finishing a food after cooking it sous vide can go beyond browning. Smoking or frying sous vide–cooked food adds more interest to your final dishes while allowing them to stay moist and tender internally.

A food cooked sous vide often has a very soft mouthfeel. Coating the food in flour, egg, and breadcrumbs and then frying it provides a crunchy texture to the exterior that can't be attained through the sous vide cooking process. This creates a nice balance with the juicy interior for truly mouthwatering food.

Smoking can be done in a dedicated smoker, with a smoke gun, or on the grill. The benefit of finishing your food this way is it combines a nice texture with an added layer of smoke flavor. While you can smoke a food before it's cooked sous vide, the food is less likely to dry out if you smoke it after cooking it.

Using smoking as the finishing step also allows the food to reach its ideal doneness before it goes in the smoker. This saves you cook time on the smoker and also gives you the option of storing the food for a day or two before smoking it.

Frying

The crunchiness developed through frying helps bring out nuances in the food beyond what can be accomplished in a hot water bath alone. This type of finish provides an interesting texture to the exterior without drying out the interior.

1 Remove the plastic bag from the water bath. Immediately place the bag into a large pot of ice water and allow to cool for 15 minutes.

2 Remove the food from the plastic bag and dry with paper towels. Once dry, season with kosher salt and any other desired seasonings.

3 Cover the food in flour. Coat the food in a mixture of equal parts egg and water. Roll the food in breadcrumbs.

4 Preheat a fryer to high. Place the food in the hot fryer and cook until it's a golden brown color, about 2 minutes. (Don't overcook.)

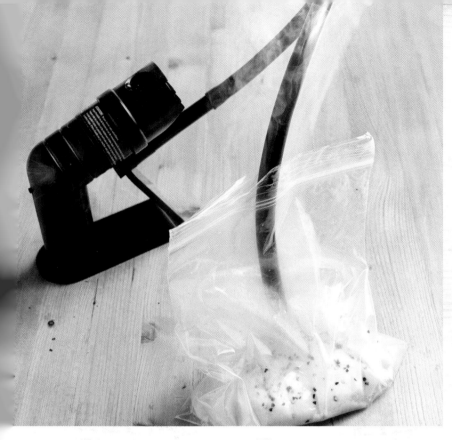

Smoking

Smoking sous vide-cooked food is a popular method for making perfect barbecue. With the sous vide process, you can cook the meat to the perfect firmness before adding the smoke flavor. Smoking after cooking sous vide helps the meat remain at its maximum juiciness.

1 Remove the plastic bag from the water bath. Immediately place the bag into a large pot of ice water and allow to cool for 30 minutes.

2 Remove the food from the plastic bag, dry with paper towels, and rub off any herbs stuck to the food (to avoid smoking them).

3 Preheat a smoker from 168°F (76°C) to 200°F (93°C), depending on the food. Place the food in the smoker and smoke for 20 minutes, until it develops a complex flavor.

4 Remove the food from the smoker and allow it to sit for 30 minutes. This allows the smoked food to shift from a blackish color to a reddish color.

TOOLS

For **frying,** you can can use a countertop fryer or a cast-iron skillet. If you plan to use a fryer, look for one with the highest heat generation, as the heat drops dramatically when food is placed in it . With a high heat output, you can ensure the heat of the oil recovers quickly. If you plan to use a cast-iron skillet, find one with high sides so the oil can cover the food.

For **smoking,** the equipment can vary widely, from a pan of smoking wood chips in the bottom of a box to multi-thousand-dollar custom trucks. You can even use a smoke gun to smoke your food, which involves pumping smoke in the plastic bag with the food and then sealing the bag for 20 minutes. However, smoking after cooking sous vide doesn't require anything elaborate; you can use whatever's easiest for you.

TROUBLESHOOTING &
tips

As you begin your journey into sous vide cooking, you may encounter some bumps in the road. These tips and tricks can help you cook like a pro and avoid many of the common pitfalls that new sous cooks often encounter.

PREP HELP #1

The best kind of prep is no prep at all. Many foods in the meat section of stores are now prepackaged in sous vide–friendly sealed plastic with an added-water solution. The solution includes a salt base that helps the meat retain moisture when cooked. These packaged foods can be put directly into the sous vide water bath and cooked without any additional prep. There are also companies that preseason foods for sous vide cooking that you simply need to seal and add to the water bath.

PREP HELP #2

Would you like to brine a food in seconds? Vacuum sealers can do much more than just seal foods in plastic bags. You can also put meat and a marinade in a bowl and place the bowl into the vacuum chamber. Once the vacuum is turned on, it pulls the air is out of the meat. When the vacuum is then released, the liquid marinade takes the place of the air that was pulled out of the meat. And poof! The meat is brined.

PREP HELP #3

Putting raw garlic in with your food can bring out some very bitter qualities, making it a poor choice for sous vide when uncooked. Asafoetida–a spice that's in the same family as garlic and onions–can stand in for raw garlic and not add that bitter taste. Simply sprinkle asafoetida on the food you'll be cooking like you would any other spice. When finished cooking, your food will taste as though you had fresh garlic sealed in with it.

SEAL HELP #1

When foods are vacuum sealed, they often end up flat around the edges. This detracts from the appearance of certain foods, such as a nice, tall steak. To help with this problem, add a couple tablespoons of a flavorless oil, such as vegetable oil, to the bag before sealing. This will help the food better retain its shape when vacuum sealed, giving you a photo-worthy final product.

COOK HELP #1

Hurry up and get cooking! With some immersion circulators, heating the water in a sous vide bath can take hours. Waiting on the water to get hot is, well, like watching a pot of water as you wait for it to boil. However, you can speed up preheating the water bath by bringing the water up to temperature in a pot on the stove. You not only help your sous vide machine, you save yourself the headache of waiting a long time for the water to reach the correct temperature.

COOK HELP #2

When green vegetables are cooked at warmer temperatures during the sous vide process, they can develop brown edges from acid development. To make them more alkaline and better able to retain their color, all you need to do is add a pinch of baking soda. You can sprinkle the baking soda in the seasoning mixture you're applying to your vegetables. Once cooked, you'll have vegetables with a green color that truly pops.

FINISH HELP #1

If you find the breading on a fried food falls off like it was never attached, that means the "glue" wasn't given time to set. When you're coating the food, first add a combination of flour and egg wash before applying the breading. The flour-egg mixture works as the glue to attach the breading to the food. In order to seal the crust, allow the coated food to set for 15 minutes after breading before adding it to the fryer.

FINISH HELP #2

Warm your torch first. While torch fuel comes in different gases, propane–available in most sporting goods stores, garden centers, and hardware stores–is the most popular and accessible type. With propane torches, the gas will not completely burn for roughly 30 seconds after it's ignited. To avoid ending up with unburned gases on your food, let the torch run for a bit before using the flame.

FINISH HELP #3

When searing your food, time is of the essence. You need an extremely hot pan so the food going onto the surface will cook quickly. You also need to make sure you have tongs or some other tool on hand to roll the food to the other side and then quickly remove it from the pan. Prepare for the searing process by preheating the pan before the food is cooked and keeping tongs next to the stove.

FINISH HELP #4

Make sure to fully dry meat before searing, grilling, or torching it. The Maillard reaction happens when the amino acids in a protein interact with a form of sugar to create browning. This develops over 200 new flavors in the food, with umami adding the most to the flavor profile. Capturing this flavor profile requires a high heat source. However, the reaction won't happen if the meat is moist on the outside, as the water will inhibit the high heat interacting with the meat. This makes drying crucial to the finishing process.

FINISH HELP #5

Grills can take a long time to preheat and often don't get as hot as necessary in order to produce the best sear on a food. To get the highest degree of heat, try placing an old cookie sheet on the grill in the area you plan to sear the food. The cookie sheet will hold the heat directly over the grill rods, leading them to become supercharged. Just before the food is ready to sear, carefully remove the sheet.

COOKING SOUS VIDE
safely

Like all other cooking methods, sous vide cooking requires you to handle and serve food in a safe manner. Following some basic safety practices will help ensure your food is cooked not only perfectly, but safely.

Poultry Temperature Guidelines

This table shows how long poultry must cook at a certain temperature in order for it to be safe to eat. These figures are based on keeping the food at that temperature for 1 second. So, for instance, to eat a safely cooked piece of chicken, you need to heat it to 165°F (74°C) for instant pasteurization or to a lower temperature for a longer time in order to achieve pasteurization.

Temperature	Time
136°F (58°C)	68.4 minutes
140°F (60°C)	27.5 minutes
145°F (63°C)	9.2 minutes
150°F (66°C)	2.8 minutes
155°F (68°C)	47.7 seconds
160°F (71°C)	14.8 seconds
165°F (74°C)	Instant

Food Safety

With any food, it's critical to cook it long enough so any foodborne pathogens are eliminated. If you don't know the necessary times and temperatures, government institutions typically provide these guidelines. In the United States, the USDA (usda.gov) has information on low long food should be cooked and at what temperatures in order to kill any bad bacteria. You'll notice the figures are based on a sliding scale, where higher temperatures kill bacteria over a shorter period of time than lower temperatures. These guidelines vary based on the specific food, so confirm what's safe for the food you're cooking before you begin.

Sealing and Storing

The safest way to cook sous vide is to seal the food and put it directly into a preheated water bath. When sealing foods in plastic, you must consider the temperature at which it's sealed, as well as how long it should be stored. Sealing food creates an environment in which there's no oxygen, meaning different anaerobic bacteria can grow. To avoid this, when initially sealing, be sure that meats and poultry are below 40°F (4°C) and that seafood is frozen. When it comes to storage, sealed foods shouldn't be stored in the refrigerator for more than 1 week. Storing them in the freezer will stop that clock and allow longer shelf life.

Safe Handling

Cross-contamination is the most common way to spread foodborne illness. People handling uncooked meat, fish, or poultry can easily spread contaminants to other locations. This means it's crucial to sanitize every surface where you've placed and worked with these items with hot water or a chlorine solution. Another major handling concern involves the packaging equipment. When putting food into plastic bags, the bags can become contaminated around the lip. When the lip of the bag is put into the sealing device, the device then becomes contaminated. To deter the spread of contaminants to future bags, wash all surfaces of your device before using it again.

broths

When making soups and sauces, the broth is the canvas onto which all other flavors are painted. By cooking sous vide, you retain the fragrant smells from the base meat, as well as develop the gelatin through the long cooking time.

Here, I've provided two different broths as your base: white and brown. The white broth has a bright, lighter flavor from the chicken. The brown broth has a richer, roasted flavor accomplished by searing the ingredients first.

SOUS VIDE BROTH TECHNIQUE

The Pho recipe in the Pork section of this book instructs you to use the broth technique shown in this spread. Simply follow the instructions for making Brown Beef Broth, substituting the ingredients here with the ingredients listed in Pho prep step 2.

White Chicken Broth

Time: 24 hours, 20 minutes
Temp: 170°F (77°C)
Yield: 2 quarts (2l)

2 lb. (1kg) chicken thighs, backs, and/or feet

½ lb. (225g) parsnips, chopped

½ lb. (225g) celery, chopped

1 lb. (450g) white onions, chopped

1 stem parsley

1 clove garlic

5 black peppercorns

½ tsp. dried thyme

1 bay leaf

2 qt. (2l) filtered water

1 Preheat the sous vide machine to 170°F (77°C).

2 Combine chicken thighs, parsnips, celery, white onions, parsley, garlic, black peppercorns, thyme, bay leaf, and filtered water in a 1-gallon (3.75l) plastic bag and seal.

3 Once the sous vide water bath has reached the desired temperature, insert the bag and allow to cook for 24 hours.

4 Remove the bag from the water bath and strain liquid through a fine-mesh sieve into a stockpot, discarding solids.

5 Use for soups and sauces. Broth can be stored for up to 4 days in the refrigerator or 6 months in the freezer.

White broths work well with poultry and fish dishes

Brown Beef Broth

Time: 24 hours, 45 minutes
Temp: 170°F (77°C)
Yield: 2 quarts (2l)

2 lb. (1kg) beef bones
1 TB. tomato paste
½ lb. (225g) carrots, chopped
1 lb. (450g) white onions, chopped
2 oz. (60ml) red wine vinegar
2 oz. (60ml) dry red wine

1 qt. (1l) water
1 stem parsley
1 clove garlic
5 black peppercorns
½ tsp. dried thyme
½ lb. (225g) celery, chopped
1 bay leaf

1 Place a large cast-iron skillet in the oven and preheat the oven to 450°F (232°C). Remove the hot skillet, add beef bones, and allow to roast for 15 minutes.

2 Add tomato paste, carrots, and white onions to the skillet. Return to the oven and allow to cook for 20 minutes.

3 Remove from the oven and scrape ingredients into a large container. Place the container into the refrigerator to cool.

4 Put the skillet on the stovetop over high heat. Add red wine vinegar and dry red wine, scraping the bottom of the skillet to loosen any browned bits. Remove from heat, add water to cool, and mix.

5 Place liquid, parsley, garlic, black peppercorns, thyme, celery, and bay leaf in a 1-gallon (3.75l) plastic bag and seal.

6 Once the sous vide water bath has reached the desired temperature, insert the bag and allow to cook for 24 hours.

7 Remove the bag from the water bath and strain liquid through fine-mesh sieve into a stockpot, discarding solids.

8 Use for soups and sauces. Broth can be stored for up to 4 days in the refrigerator or 6 months in the freezer.

Brown broths are richer in flavor than white broths and are often used with hearty meat dishes

infusions

Low-temperature infusions combine a primary ingredient with seasonings. For instance, oils can be pumped full of herbal flavors, and creams can be enhanced with floral components. Sous vide makes this process a snap.

OILS AND BUTTER

These flavored oils can be used for high-heat applications (such as searing), while the butter can be used as a nice topper for any dish.

Mint Butter

Time: 1 hour, 10 minutes
Temp: 135°F (57°C)
Yield: 1 pound (450g)

1 lb. (450g) whole butter
½ cup mint leaves, packed

1 Preheat the sous vide machine to 135°F (57°C).

2 Combine whole butter and mint leaves in a 1-quart (1l) plastic bag and seal.

3 Insert the plastic bag and allow to cook for 1 hour.

4 Remove the bag from the water bath. Use immediately or store in the freezer for up to 1 year.

Garlic Oil

Time: 3 hours, 10 minutes
Temp: 135°F (57°C)
Yield: 32 ounces (1l)

32 oz. (1l) extra-virgin olive oil
10 garlic cloves

1 Preheat the sous vide machine to 135°F (57°C).

2 Combine extra-virgin olive oil and garlic cloves in a 1-quart (1l) plastic bag and seal.

3 Insert the plastic bag and allow to cook for 3 hours.

4 Remove the bag from the water bath. Use immediately or store in the freezer for up to 1 year.

Thyme Oil

Time: 3 hours, 10 minutes
Temp: 135°F (57°C)
Yield: 8 ounces (237ml)

8 oz. (237ml) extra-virgin olive oil
1 TB. dried thyme

1 Preheat the sous vide machine to 135°F (57°C).

2 Combine extra-virgin olive oil and thyme in a 1-quart (1l) plastic bag and seal.

3 Insert the plastic bag and allow to cook for 3 hours.

4 Remove the bag from the water bath. Use immediately or store in the freezer for up to 1 year.

With infused creams, you can go beyond using them as a thickener and give dishes a sweet or savory boost.

Basil Cream

Time: 2 hours, 10 minutes
Temp: 165°F (74°C)
Yield: 16 ounces (473ml)

16 oz. (473ml) heavy whipping cream
8 basil leaves

1 Preheat the sous vide machine to 165°F (74°C).

2 Combine heavy whipping cream and basil in a 1-quart (1l) plastic bag and seal.

3 Insert the plastic bag and allow to cook for 2 hours.

4 Remove the bag from the water bath. Use immediately or store in the refrigerator for up to 1 month.

Mushroom Cream

Time: 2 hours, 10 minutes
Temp: 165°F (74°C)
Yield: 16 ounces (473ml)

16 oz. (473ml) heavy whipping cream
¼ cup shiitake mushrooms, chopped

1 Preheat the sous vide machine to 165°F (74°C).

2 Combine heavy whipping cream and shiitake mushrooms in a 1-quart (1l) plastic bag and seal.

3 Insert the plastic bag and allow to cook for 2 hours.

4 Remove the bag from the water bath. Use immediately or store in the refrigerator for up to 1 month.

Lavender Cream

Time: 2 hours, 10 minutes
Temp: 165°F (74°C)
Yield: 8 ounces (237ml)

8 oz. (237ml) heavy whipping cream
8 lavender flower stems

1 Preheat the sous vide machine to 165°F (74°C).

2 Combine heavy whipping cream and lavender in a 1-quart (1l) plastic bag and seal.

3 Insert the plastic bag and allow to cook for 2 hours.

4 Remove the bag from the water bath. Use immediately or store in the refrigerator for up to 1 month.

SOUS VIDE COCKTAIL INFUSIONS

You can infuse about anything using your sous vide machine, including alcohol! For **Vanilla-Orange Vodka,** combine 16 ounces (473ml) vodka, 1 orange zest, and 1 vanilla bean in 1-quart (1l) glass canning jars and place in a 130°F (54°C) water bath for 2 hours; strain and serve. For an **Old-Fashioned,** combine 16 ounces (473ml) whiskey, 1 orange zest, 3 ounces (85g) granulated sugar, and 4 luxardo cherries in 1-quart (1l) glass canning jars and place in a 130°F (54°C) water bath for 2 hours; strain and serve. For **Limoncello,** combine 10 lemon zests, 1 (25-oz.; 750ml) bottle vodka, 1 cup granulated sugar, and ½ cup water in a 1-quart (1l) plastic bag and place in a 135°F (57°C) water bath for 3 hours; strain into a decorative bottle and place in the freezer for 1 week before serving as a cold beverage.

Vegetables & Fruits

VEGETABLE & FRUIT
basics

One of the biggest enemies of fruits and vegetables–or any food–is oxygen, which permeates the food and starts to break down molecules. Cooked the traditional way, where they're very much exposed to oxygen, fruits and vegetables become dull in color. Vacuum packaging them for sous vide dramatically slows the breakdown of the molecules in fruits and vegetables, leading to bright colors that can give a pop to entrées or side dishes.

Vegetables cooked sous vide tend to have higher vitamin content compared to those steamed or simmered in water. By holding all the nutrients in the bag, they aren't diluted in the water that surrounds them. Couple that with cooking them at lower temperatures, and you keep the vitamins from breaking out of the cell structure.

When it comes to fruits, most have a certain amount of pectin in them. This pectin gives food a firmer structure. However, pectin begins to break down at 185°F (85°C). If you cook fruits sous vide, however, you can stop that breakdown, leading to a firmer texture than what traditional cooking provides.

Green beans cooked sous vide

Green beans cooked traditionally

Because vegetables have to cook at a much higher temperature than meats, you may think you can't have a one-bag meal. However, if you **sous vide the vegetables first**, you can then add them to the meat that needs to cook. As long as the cooking temperatures stay below 183°F (84°C), the vegetables won't cook any further.

When preparing...
Add an acidic ingredient (such as orange juice) to bags containing red vegetables. In the presence of acid, these vegetables become even redder during the cooking process. Some fruits, such as apples and peaches, will brown quickly when they're cut. Dipping them in lemon juice helps slow down this browning.

When finishing...
You can simply remove the fruits or vegetables from their sous vide bags, divide among plates, and serve as is! Other options include simmering or boiling them with other ingredients when making soup, browning them in the oven, putting them in the blender for a purée, or (in the case of potatoes) frying them for a couple minutes.

VEGETABLE & FRUIT
times & temperatures

	COOKING TEMP	TIME	SIZE/NUMBER
Apples	185°F (85°C)	1 hour	2, peeled, cored, and diced
Artichokes	182°F (83°C)	30 minutes	1 large
Asparagus	190°F (88°C)	4 minutes	½ lb. (225g), woody ends removed
Baby beets	182°F (83°C)	1 hour	1 lb. (450g)
Baby carrots	185°F (85°C)	1 hour, 15 minutes	1 lb. (450g)
Cauliflower	183°F (84°C)	2 hours	1 lb. (450g), trimmed
Corn	185°F (85°C)	2 hours	5 ears
Fennel	185°F (85°C)	1 hour	1 lb. (450g), cut into 1-in. (2.5cm) pieces
Kidney beans	190°F (88°C)	6 hours	4 oz. (110g)
Leeks	185°F (85°C)	20 minutes	1 large, green tops removed and whites diced
Navy beans	190°F (88°C)	6 hours	4 oz. (110g)
Pearl onions	185°F (85°C)	1 hour, 30 minutes	1 lb. (450g), peeled
Pickled beets	190°F (88°C)	40 minutes	12 oz. (340g), cut into ½-in. (1.25cm) slices ⅓ inch (.75cm) thick
Radishes	182°F (83°C)	45 minutes	1 lb. (450g), cut in half lengthwise
Red cabbage	183°F (84°C)	45 minutes	1 small, outer leaves removed, cored, and thinly sliced
Red potatoes	190°F (88°C)	1 hour	1 lb. (450g)
Russet potatoes	190°F (88°C)	1 hour	2½ lb. (1.1kg), cut into french-fry shape
	194°F (90°C)	25 minutes	1 lb. (450g), peeled and sliced 1 in. (2.5cm) thick
Shiitake mushrooms	185°F (85°C)	dried: 45 minutes; fresh: 20 minutes	dried: 1 oz. (25g); fresh: 1 lb. (450g)
Sweet potatoes	185°F (85°C)	1 hour	1 lb. (450g), peeled and diced small
Turnips	185°F (85°C)	2 hours	1 small, peeled and diced small

Pickling is easy with sous vide! This recipe walks you through how to pickle beets, which enhances their naturally sweet flavor.

pickled
VEGETABLES

 2 hours

 190°F (88°C)

4 servings

12 oz. (340g) beets, cut into ½-in. (1.25cm) slices

½ serrano pepper, seeds removed

1 garlic clove, diced

⅔ cup white wine vinegar

⅔ cup filtered water

2 TB. pickling spice

PREP AND SEAL — 20 minutes

1 Preheat the sous vide machine to 190°F (88°C).

2 Place beets, serrano pepper, and garlic in a 1-quart (1l) canning jar. Set aside.

3 In a medium stockpot, combine white wine vinegar, filtered water, and pickling spice and bring to a boil over high heat.

4 Remove stockpot from heat and strain mixture over beets to fill the glass jar. Seal the jar.

COOK — 40 minutes

1 Once the sous vide water bath has reached the desired temperature, insert the jar of beets and allow to cook for 40 minutes.

2 Remove the jar from the water bath.

FINISH — 1 hour

1 Allow the jar of beets to cool at room temperature for 1 hour.

2 Serve immediately or store in the refrigerator for up to 12 months.

You can **change the item being pickled** to whatever you'd like. At the temperature mentioned in the recipe, cook root vegetables for 40 minutes and other tender vegetables for 10 minutes.

PREP AND SEAL 5 minutes

1 Preheat the sous vide machine to 185°F (85°C).

2 Put sweet potatoes and 1 tablespoon canola oil in a 1-quart (1l) plastic bag and seal.

COOK 2 hours, 5 minutes

1 Once the sous vide water bath has reached the desired temperature, insert the plastic bag of sweet potatoes and oil and allow to cook for 1 hour. Remove the plastic bag from the water bath and set aside.

2 In a 1-gallon (3.75l) plastic bag, combine filtered water, ginger, garlic head, dried shiitake mushrooms, and white miso. Seal.

3 Insert the plastic bag of dried mushrooms into the 185°F (85°C) water bath and allow to cook for 45 minutes. Remove the plastic bag from the water bath and set aside.

4 In a large saucepan over medium-high heat, cook fresh shiitake mushrooms in remaining 2 tablespoons canola oil until water has cooked out of them and they're browned, about 8 minutes.

5 In 1-gallon (3.75l) plastic bag, combine cooked shiitake mushrooms, yellow onion, leek whites, and garlic cloves. Seal.

6 Insert the plastic bag of cooked mushrooms into the 185°F (85°C) water bath and allow to cook for 20 minutes. Remove the plastic bag from the water bath and set aside.

FINISH 30 minutes

1 Preheat an oven to 400°F (204°C).

2 Remove sweet potatoes from the plastic bag, discarding liquid.

3 Place ½ of sweet potatoes on a sheet pan. Insert the sheet pan into the oven and allow to cook for 7 minutes, or until browned. Set aside.

4 Meanwhile, place remaining ½ of sweet potatoes in a food processor and purée until smooth.

5 Strain the plastic bag of dried mushrooms into a large stockpot, discarding any solids. Add puréed sweet potatoes.

6 Add ingredients from the plastic bag of cooked mushrooms to the pot and bring to a boil over high heat. Season to taste with tamari.

7 Divide ramen noodles among the serving bowls. Pour hot broth over noodles.

8 Top each with green onions, soft-boiled egg half, and roasted sweet potatoes and serve.

Ramen broth is a combination of sweet, salty, and umami. By cooking those combinations in separate sous vide bags, you get a mouthwatering layering of flavor in the final product.

VEGETABLE
ramen

 2 hours, 40 minutes

 185°F (85°C)

 8 servings

2 sweet potatoes (about 1 lb.; 450g), peeled and diced small

3 TB. canola oil

1½ qt. (1.4l) filtered water

1 (2-in.; 5cm) piece fresh ginger, peeled and chopped

1 head garlic, minced

1 oz. (25g) dried shiitake mushrooms

¼ cup white or yellow miso

1 lb. (450g) fresh shiitake mushrooms, sliced

1 yellow onion, diced

1 large leek, green tops removed and whites diced

4 cloves garlic, chopped

Tamari

1½ lb. (680g) fresh or cooked ramen noodles

2 green onions, thinly sliced

4 soft-boiled eggs, sliced in half

Summer sweet corn is a food that's very flavorful all on its own. By cooking this soup in bags, you help retain the wonderful aroma and delicate sweetness of the corn.

CORN
soup

 2 hours, 50 minutes

 185°F (85°C)

 8 servings

5 ears corn

1½ qt. (1.4l) filtered water

1 TB. butter

2 tsp. kosher salt

1 tsp. granulated sugar

1 cup heavy whipping cream

PREP AND SEAL — 20 minutes

1 Preheat the sous vide machine to 185°F (85°C).

2 Using a knife, cut corn off of cobs.

3 Put corn cobs and filtered water in a 1-gallon (3.75l) plastic bag and seal. Set aside.

4 In a separate 1-gallon (3.75l) plastic bag, put corn kernels, butter, kosher salt, and sugar. Seal and set aside in the refrigerator.

COOK — 2 hours

1 Once the sous vide water bath has reached the desired temperature, insert the plastic bag of corn cobs and allow to cook for 2 hours.

2 With 20 minutes left for corn cobs, insert the plastic bag of corn kernels with the other bag in the 185°F (85°C) water bath.

3 Remove both plastic bags from the water bath.

FINISH — 30 minutes

1 Strain liquid from the plastic bag of corn kernels into a large stockpot, setting aside solids.

2 Add heavy whipping cream and allow to simmer over medium heat until liquid has evaporated by half, about 15 minutes. Remove from heat.

3 Strain liquid from the plastic bag of corn cobs into the stockpot, discarding corn cobs, and stir to combine.

4 Add corn kernels to the stockpot and serve immediately.

Hearty vegetable soup warms the soul and helps fight off the chill of winter. This recipe uses the sous vide technique for cooking root vegetables so you get a nicely textured soup.

VEGETABLE
soup

 2 hours, 30 minutes

 185°F (85°C)

 10 servings

1 small turnip, peeled and diced small

1 small carrot, peeled and diced small

1 small parsnip, peeled and diced small

½ medium red onion, peeled and diced small

1 stalk celery, diced small

1 tsp. garlic powder

4 sprigs fresh thyme, stem on

1 bay leaf

½ tsp. cracked black peppercorns

1½ qt. (1.4l) chicken stock or broth

1 TB. kosher salt

PREP AND SEAL   10 minutes

1 Preheat the sous vide machine to 185°F (85°C).

2 Combine turnip, carrot, parsnip, red onion, celery, garlic powder, thyme, bay leaf, cracked black peppercorns, and chicken stock in a 1-gallon (1l) plastic bag and seal.

COOK   2 hours

1 Once the sous vide water bath has reached the desired temperature, insert the plastic bag of broth and seasoned vegetables and allow to cook for 2 hours.

2 Remove the plastic bag from the water bath.

FINISH   20 minutes

1 Open the plastic bag and remove thyme stems and bay leaf.

2 Strain liquid from the plastic bag of seasoned vegetables into a large stockpot, setting aside vegetables.

3 Add kosher salt to liquid and allow to simmer over medium heat for 10 minutes. Remove from heat.

4 Add vegetables to the stockpot and stir to combine. Serve immediately.

This take on the popular New York salad combines savory chicken, fresh apple, crunchy walnuts, and sweet grapes with a mayonnaise-based dressing.

WALDORF
salad

 2 hours, 45 minutes

 145°F (63°C)

 4 servings

2 (5-oz..; 140g) boneless and skinless chicken breasts

½ tsp. large-grind black pepper

1 TB. corn oil

1 Granny Smith apple, cored and diced

1 tsp. lime juice

½ cup red grapes, cut in half

1 rib celery, diced

⅓ cup mayonnaise

2 tsp. chardonnay wine

1 tsp. Dijon mustard

1 TB. kosher salt

1 head Romaine lettuce

½ cup walnuts, chopped and toasted

PREP AND SEAL　　　　　　　　　　15 minutes

1 Preheat the sous vide machine to 145°F (63°C).

2 Season chicken breasts with black pepper.

3 Put seasoned chicken breasts and corn oil in a 1-quart (1l) plastic bag and seal.

COOK　　　　　　　　　　　　　　2 hours

1 Once the sous vide water bath has reached the desired temperature, insert the plastic bag of seasoned chicken breasts and corn oil and allow to cook for 2 hours.

2 Remove the plastic bag from the water bath and set aside to cool.

FINISH　　　　　　　　　　　　30 minutes

1 Place Granny Smith apple slices in a large bowl. Add lime juice and toss.

2 Add red grapes and celery and stir to combine.

3 In a small bowl, combine mayonnaise, chardonnay wine, and Dijon mustard. Add to fruit mixture and toss.

4 Remove chicken breasts from the plastic bag, discarding liquid, and dice. In a medium bowl, place diced chicken and kosher salt and toss.

5 Add seasoned chicken to rest of salad and toss to combine.

6 Divide Romaine lettuce among salad bowls. Spoon salad on top of lettuce, sprinkle with toasted walnuts, and serve.

In this fresh, summery salad, peppery arugula is topped with sweet baby beets, tangy goat cheese, and crunchy almonds.

BABY BEET
salad

 1 hour, 30 minutes

 182°F (83°C)

 4 servings

1 lb. (450g) baby beets
1 tsp. kosher salt
Juice of 1 orange
½ cup baby arugula
¼ lb. (115g) goat cheese
2 mandarin oranges, cut into wedges
¼ cup slivered almonds

PREP AND SEAL — 20 minutes

1 Preheat the sous vide machine to 182°F (83°C).

2 Completely clean baby beets of any dirt and remove stems. Cut beets in half lengthwise.

3 Season beet halves with kosher salt.

4 Put seasoned beet halves and orange juice in a 1-quart (1l) plastic bag and seal.

COOK — 1 hour

1 Once the sous vide water bath has reached the desired temperature, insert the plastic bag of beet halves and orange juice and allow to cook for 1 hour.

2 Remove the plastic bag from the water bath.

FINISH — 10 minutes

1 Remove beef halves from the bag, discarding orange juice.

2 Divide baby arugula among plates. Top with beet halves, goat cheese, mandarin orange wedges, and almonds and serve.

If you have trouble finding baby beets at your local grocery store, **feel free to substitute regular beets.** Note that you'll need to increase the cook time to 1 hour, 30 minutes.

Trying to cook asparagus perfectly is a challenge, as the tip cooks more quickly than the stalk. Enter sous vide, which gives you a consistently cooked gourmet vegetable.

asparagus

 11 minutes

 190°F (88°C)

 2 servings

½ lb. (225g) asparagus, woody ends removed
1 tsp. garlic powder
1 TB. whole butter
½ tsp. sea salt
¼ tsp. ground black pepper

PREP AND SEAL   **5 minutes**

1 Preheat the sous vide machine to 190°F (88°C).

2 Combine asparagus, garlic powder, whole butter, sea salt, and black pepper in a 1-gallon (3.75l) plastic bag and seal, keeping asparagus in a single layer.

COOK   **4 minutes**

1 Once the sous vide water bath has reached the desired temperature, insert the plastic bag of seasoned asparagus and allow to cook for 4 minutes.

2 Remove the plastic bag from the water bath.

FINISH   **2 minutes**

1 Remove asparagus from the bag, discarding the rest.

2 Divide asparagus between plates and serve.

Whole butter contains milk solids, water, and oil. If you'd like to **cook a vegetarian version,** you can use a good-quality sunflower oil along with 1 teaspoon vegetable stock in place of the whole butter.

Cauliflower is a flavorful vegetable that can be steamed, sautéed, or even whipped like a mashed potato. This recipe cooks everything together before whipping to retain the rich flavors.

whipped
CAULIFLOWER

 2 hours, 15 minutes

 183°F (84°C)

4 servings

1 lb. (450g) cauliflower, trimmed
½ tsp. garlic powder
1 tsp. kosher salt
1 TB. butter
1 TB. heavy whipping cream

PREP AND SEAL — 5 minutes

1 Preheat the sous vide machine to 183°F (84°C).

2 Combine cauliflower, garlic powder, kosher salt, butter, and heavy whipping cream in a 1-gallon (3.75l) plastic bag and seal.

COOK — 2 hours

1 Once the sous vide water bath has reached the desired temperature, insert the plastic bag of cauliflower and allow to cook for 2 hours.

2 Remove the plastic bag from the water bath.

FINISH — 10 minutes

1 Pour contents of the bag into a blender. Starting on a slow speed and going progressively faster, purée until smooth.

2 Season to taste and serve like you would mashed potatoes.

If simply puréeing the cauliflower doesn't give you the fluffy, whipped consistency you desire, place the puréed contents in a large bowl and **use an electric mixer on a medium setting** for a minute or two.

Bean salad lasts a long time and tastes good cold, warm, or hot. Cooking the beans in a canning jar makes it that much easier to store leftovers.

BEAN
salad

 30 hours, 20 minutes

 190°F (88°C)

 6 servings

4 oz. (110g) dry navy beans

4 oz. (110g) dry kidney beans

4 cups water

1 shallot, minced

1 tsp. kosher salt

1 tsp. granulated sugar

1 TB. champagne or white wine vinegar

3 TB. extra-virgin olive oil

PREP AND SEAL   10 minutes

1 Preheat the sous vide machine to 190°F (88°C).

2 Place dry navy beans, dry kidney beans, and 3 cups water into a 1-quart (1l) glass canning jar and seal with the lid.

COOK   6 hours

1 Once the sous vide water bath has reached the desired temperature, insert the jar of beans and allow to cook for 2 hours.

2 Remove the lid from the jar and add shallot, kosher salt, sugar, and remaining 1 cup water. Seal with the lid, return to the 190°F (88°C) water bath, and allow to cook for 4 hours.

3 Remove the jar from the water bath.

FINISH   24 hours, 10 minutes

1 Allow the jar to sit at room temperature for 1 hour.

2 Remove the lid from the jar and add champagne vinegar and extra-virgin olive oil.

3 Seal the jar with the lid and then shake it to evenly disperse all its contents.

4 Place the jar in the refrigerator for 24 hours.

5 Pour bean salad into a large bowl and serve.

PREP AND SEAL   5 minutes

1 Preheat the sous vide machine to 185°F (85°C).

2 Combine baby carrots, whole butter, honey, kosher salt, and cardamom in a 1-quart (1l) plastic bag and seal.

COOK   1 hour, 15 minutes

1 Once the sous vide water bath has reached the desired temperature, insert the plastic bag of baby carrots and glaze and allow to cook for 1 hour, 15 minutes.

2 Remove the plastic bag from the water bath.

FINISH   10 minutes

1 Strain glaze from the bag through a fine-mesh sieve into a medium bowl and set aside to add back to carrots or save for other uses.

2 Remove carrots from the bag, pour excess glaze over them (if using), and serve as is or seasoned to your liking.

Cooking carrots sous vide helps soften them and retains their rich orange color. The butter, honey, and cardamom glaze adds a sweetness that will make you want seconds.

GLAZED
carrots

 1 hour, 30 minutes

 185°F (85°C)

 4 servings

1 lb. (450g) baby carrots
4 TB. whole butter
1 TB. honey
¼ tsp. kosher salt
¼ tsp. ground cardamom

Vegetables like carrots have pectin in them, which helps them hold together their cell structure. Because pectin starts to melt at 182°F (83°C), **most vegetables are cooked at 183°F (84°C) or warmer** to break down that pectin, thereby making them softer.

Many people avoid artichokes because of the long cooking time and the high amount of waste. Sous vide cooks artichokes more quickly and wastes far less of the edible portion.

artichoke

 55 minutes

 182°F (83°C)

2 servings

1 artichoke
1 tsp. sea salt
1 clove garlic, sautéed
2 TB. butter

PREP AND SEAL | 15 minutes

1 Preheat the sous vide machine to 182°F (83°C).

2 Peel off outer leaves and stem of artichoke. Cut artichoke in half from bloom end to stem end. Season interior with sea salt and garlic.

3 Combine seasoned artichoke halves and butter in a 1-quart (1l) plastic bag and seal.

COOK | 30 minutes

1 Once the sous vide water bath has reached the desired temperature, insert the plastic bag of seasoned artichoke halves and butter and allow to cook for 30 minutes.

2 Remove the plastic bag from the water bath.

FINISH | 10 minutes

1 Remove artichoke halves from the bag, discarding liquid.

2 Remove choke (fuzzy center) from each half with a spoon and serve.

You may notice spines situated at the top of artichoke petals. To avoid pricking your fingers, **it's a good idea to get rid of them.** Take a sharp pair of kitchen scissors, cut across the petal, and discard the spines.

Pearl onions are little bundles of flavor that are great on their own as a side dish or alongside other vegetables, such as carrots or green beans.

PEARL
onions

 1 hour, 50 minutes

 185°F (85°C)

 4 servings

1 lb. (450g) pearl onions, peeled
1 slice bacon, cooked and crumbled
   (optional)
1 stem thyme, leaves only

PREP AND SEAL	10 minutes
1 Preheat the sous vide machine to 185°F (85°C).	2 Combine pearl onions, bacon (if using), and thyme in a 1-quart (1l) plastic bag and seal.

COOK	1 hour, 30 minutes
1 Once the sous vide water bath has reached the desired temperature, insert the plastic bag of pearl onions and allow to cook for 1 hour, 30 minutes.	2 Remove the plastic bag from the water bath.

FINISH	10 minutes
1 Strain any liquid out of the bag and discard.	2 Divide pearl onions among plates and serve.

You can also use the sous vide process to make **pearl onion confit.** Add 1 cup of extra-virgin olive oil along with the other ingredients during prep, and you'll end up with a tasty topper for sandwiches.

PREP AND SEAL   20 minutes

1 Preheat the sous vide machine to 194°F (90°C).

2 In a large bowl, combine water, kosher salt, sugar, and baking soda until all solids are dissolved in water; this forms a brine.

3 Place russet potato fries in a single layer in two 1-gallon (3.75l) plastic bags. Add enough brine to equal weight of fries, making sure to cover all fries, and seal.

COOK   25 minutes

1 Once the sous vide water bath has reached the desired temperature, insert the plastic bags of fries and allow to cook for 25 minutes.

2 Remove the plastic bags from the water bath.

FINISH   1 hour, 40 minutes

1 Preheat a fryer to 260°F (127°C). Remove fries from brine and place on a cooling rack to dry, about 20 minutes.

2 Place dried fries in the fryer and allow to cook for 8 minutes to set outside.

3 Transfer fries to the freezer to and allow to completely freeze, about 1 hour.

4 Preheat a fryer to 375°F (191°C). When the fryer has reached the desired temperature, add fries and allow to cook for 2 minutes.

5 Remove fries from the fryer and serve.

If you're looking for the most glorious french fries possible, sous vide's here to help. These fries have a really crispy exterior and a wonderfully light and fluffy interior.

FRENCH
fries

 2 hours, 25 minutes

 194°F (90°C)

 10 servings

2 qt. (2l) water

2 TB. kosher salt

1 tsp. granulated sugar

1 tsp. baking soda

2¹/₂ lb. (1.1kg) russet potatoes, cut into french-fry shape ¹/₃ in. (.75cm) thick

Freezing the fries after frying them the first time causes the water molecules to expand and burst cell walls in the potatoes. This process ensures an extra-crunchy texture after the fries are cooked a second time.

To cook confit means to poach in an oil. This recipe cooks red potatoes in a butter-oil mixture, which results in the creamiest potatoes you can imagine.

confit
POTATOES

 1 hour, 20 minutes

 190°F (88°C)

 4 servings

1 lb. (450g) small red potatoes
1 tsp. kosher salt
¼ tsp. ground white pepper
1 tsp. fresh rosemary, chopped
2 TB. whole butter
1 TB. corn oil

PREP AND SEAL — 15 minutes

1 Preheat the sous vide machine to 190°F (88°C).

2 Cut red potatoes in half. Season potato halves with kosher salt, white pepper, and rosemary.

3 Combine seasoned potato halves, whole butter, and corn oil in a 1-quart (1l) plastic bag—ensuring potato halves are in a single layer—and seal.

COOK — 1 hour

1 Once the sous vide water bath has reached the desired temperature, insert the plastic bag of seasoned potato halves and butter-oil mixture and allow to cook for 1 hour.

2 Remove the plastic bag from the water bath.

FINISH — 5 minutes

1 Place potatoes and butter-oil mixture in a large bowl, or divide among plates.

2 Serve potatoes as a side dish. They can also be seared as desired before serving.

Confit potatoes are nicely adaptable to any flavor combination you like. For instance, if you're **serving them with an Indian-inspired dish, include coriander and turmeric** in the bag for a complementary taste.

Fennel has a licorice-like smell and a fresh flavor reminiscent of summer. Puréed fennel is great as a sauce for other foods or even as a spread for sandwiches.

fennel
PURÉE

 1 hour, 15 minutes

 185°F (85°C)

 4 servings

1 lb. (450g) fennel bulbs, cut into 1-in. (2.5cm) pieces
1 tsp. extra-virgin olive oil
¼ tsp. kosher salt
¼ tsp. granulated sugar

PREP AND SEAL   5 minutes

1 Preheat the sous vide machine to 185°F (85°C).

2 Combine fennel, extra-virgin olive oil, kosher salt, and sugar in a 1-gallon (3.75l) plastic bag and seal.

COOK   1 hour

1 Once the sous vide water bath has reached the desired temperature, insert the plastic bag of seasoned fennel and allow to cook for 1 hour.

2 Remove the plastic bag from the water bath.

FINISH   10 minutes

1 Pour ingredients from the bag into a blender. Purée on high until mixture is smooth.

2 Serve fennel purée as a sauce or spread.

You can **turn this purée into a delicious soup** with a few simple changes. In a stockpot, combine 2 cups vegetable stock and 1 cup heavy cream and allow to cook over medium heat for 10 to 15 minutes. Pour the hot liquid into the blender along with the ingredients from the bag and purée as directed.

Instead of cooking these potatoes in water–which can cause them to lose flavor–they're cooked with butter and cream. This gives you a deliciously decadent purée.

potato
PURÉE

 1 hour, 15 minutes

 190°F (88°C)

 4 servings

1 lb. (450g) russet potatoes, peeled and sliced 1 in. (2.5cm) thick

8 TB. butter

½ cup heavy cream

1 tsp. kosher salt

PREP AND SEAL	5 minutes
1 Preheat the sous vide machine to 190°F (88°C).	2 Combine russet potatoes, butter, heavy cream, and kosher salt in a 1-gallon (3.75l) plastic bag and seal.

COOK	1 hour
1 Once the sous vide water bath has reached the desired temperature, insert the plastic bag of potatoes and butter-cream mixture and allow to cook for 1 hour.	2 Remove the plastic bag from the water bath.

FINISH	10 minutes
1 Pass ingredients from the bag through a food mill and into a large bowl. Whisk simply to incorporate. (If you don't have a food mill, you can use a mixer or ricer.)	2 Serve potato purée as a side with any meat dish.

If you decide to use a mixer instead of a food mill, **you should be especially careful not to overmix the potatoes.** If they're overworked, they'll lose their fluffiness, resulting in an unpleasantly sticky texture.

PREP AND SEAL		**5 minutes**

1 Preheat the sous vide machine to 185°F (85°C).

2 Combine tart apples, Madras curry powder, and coconut cream in a 1-gallon (3.75l) plastic bag and seal.

COOK		**1 hour**

1 Once the sous vide water bath has reached the desired temperature, insert the plastic bag of seasoned apples and liquid and allow to cook for 1 hour.

2 Remove the plastic bag from the water bath.

FINISH		**5 minutes**

1 Place apples and liquid in a large bowl, or divide among plates.

2 Serve as a side dish with meats or other vegetable-based dishes.

The light spice of curry and the sweetness of apples are a glorious combination. Cooking the apples sous vide ensures they aren't mushy, so you have a great side dish.

CURRIED
apples

 1 hour, 10 minutes

 185°F (85°C)

 4 servings

2 tart apples, peeled, cored, and sliced
1 TB. Madras curry powder
2 TB. coconut cream

To ensure you have an even amount of servings, after peeling and coring the apples, **cut each into 20 ¼-inch (.5cm) slices.** This will give you 10 apple slices, or about ½ cup, for each serving.

Sometimes sous vide isn't about cooking; it's simply about vacuum sealing. This method takes the air out of watermelon, concentrating the flavor.

COMPRESSED
water melon

 35 minutes

 none

 10 servings

1 seedless watermelon

PREP AND SEAL   30 minutes

1 Peel watermelon and cut meat into 1×1×½-inch (2.5×2.5×1.25cm) pieces.

2 Place watermelon pieces in a single layer in a 1-gallon (3.75l) plastic bag.

3 If you're using a bag sealer, seal watermelon pieces into the bag. If you're using a vacuum chamber, pull a 99.9 percent vacuum.

4 Repeat the sealing process three more times for the bag sealer or two more times for the vacuum chamber, cutting open the top of the bag and starting over each time.

FINISH   5 minutes

1 Remove watermelon pieces from the bag.

2 Enjoy watermelon pieces on their own or use them to make a dessert sushi.

The compression process also lends itself well to **infusing flavors into the watermelon.** Add a vinaigrette, yogurt, sauce, or any other liquid flavoring you'd like to the bag before you begin compressing the watermelon.

Braising radishes helps mute the heat associated with them while bringing out their natural flavors. The sous vide process takes the worry out of overcooking this dish.

BRAISED
radishes

 1 hour

182°F (83°C)

4 servings

1 lb. (450g) radishes, cut in half lengthwise

3 TB. butter

½ tsp. sea salt

1 Preheat the sous vide machine to 182°F (83°C).

2 Combine radish halves, butter, and sea salt in a 1-gallon (3.75l) plastic bag and seal.

1 Once the sous vide water bath has reached the desired temperature, insert the plastic bag of seasoned radishes and allow to cook for 45 minutes.

2 Remove the plastic bag from the water bath.

1 Strain liquid from radishes and discard.

2 Serve radishes as a side dish or as an appetizer.

Balsamic or red wine vinegar can add some brightness to these radishes. If you're looking for extra flavor and texture, you can also **toss braised radishes with bacon or shallots.**

Many people tend to associate cabbage with foul smells. However, red cabbage cooked sous vide gives this dish the pleasant aroma and taste of sweet plum and grapes.

RED
cabbage

 1 hour, 10 minutes

 183°F (84°C)

 8 to 10 servings

½ tsp. kosher salt

¼ tsp. ground black pepper

¼ tsp. garlic powder

½ cinnamon stick

1 TB. grape jelly

1 small red cabbage, outer leaves removed, cored, and thinly sliced

1 tart apple, peeled, cored, and diced

1 small yellow onion, peeled and diced

Juice of 1 lemon

2 TB. butter

PREP AND SEAL   15 minutes

1 Preheat the sous vide machine to 183°F (84°C).

2 In a large bowl, combine kosher salt, black pepper, garlic powder, cinnamon, grape jelly, red cabbage, apple, yellow onion, lemon juice, and butter.

3 Place cabbage mixture in two 1-gallon (3.75l) plastic bags, making sure cabbage is spread out in a single layer, and seal.

COOK   45 minutes

1 Once the sous vide water bath has reached the desired temperature, insert the plastic bag of seasoned cabbage and allow to cook for 45 minutes.

2 Remove the plastic bag from the water bath.

FINISH   10 minutes

1 In a large bowl, combine contents of both bags.

2 Season to taste, if desired, and serve as a side dish for an entrée.

Because of the combination of sweet and sour from the jelly, apple, onion, and lemon, this form of red cabbage **pairs well with poultry and pork dishes.**

Poultry

POULTRY
basics

Chicken cooked sous vide

Chicken cooked traditionally

One of the main concerns when cooking protein is salmonella–a bacteria responsible for foodborne illness. This harmful bacteria can be instantly eradicated at a temperature of 163°F (73°C) in traditional cooking. However, having to cook poultry to such a high temperature releases a lot of moisture, leaving the protein dry.

Cooking sous vide allows you to kill off salmonella by using longer time periods at lower temperatures. So instead of needing to raise the temperature to 163°F (73°C) to kill salmonella, you can reach the same bacteria-killing levels by cooking as low as 140°F (60°C) for 1 hour. This makes for a much juicier piece of meat that's still free of harmful bacteria.

This groundbreaking method for cooking poultry allows you to eat poultry that has a little pink color in the flesh. However, because you may be used to a drier piece of meat, it may take a few times of tasting the poultry to start to feel comfortable eating it this way. Play with different temperatures and times, and you'll dial into your favorite taste preferences over time.

Be sure to **set a timer when cooking poultry sous vide.** While it can be cooked for a longer time than when using traditional methods, poultry—especially white meat—doesn't do well if left in a sous vide bath for too long. When that happens, the poultry proteins start to break down and become mushy.

When preparing...
Brine poultry in salt or sugar solutions. This gives you a more flexible timetable before the protein dries out while cooking. If you know you're going to be away and can't pull the turkey breast out of the sous vide bath in time, brining will help retain moisture and give you some extra cook time.

When finishing...
With chicken, you can dice it up before adding it to a salad, dredge and fry it, or put it on the grill or smoker. Turkey can be served as is or seared in a pan or with a blowtorch. Duck is great right out of the bag or mixed with fat and made into rillettes.

times & temperatures

	COOKING TEMP	TIME	SIZE/NUMBER
Chicken breasts (diced)	147°F (64°C)	1 hour	2
Chicken breasts (whole)	145°F (63°C), 147°F (64°C), or 150°F (66°C)	1 hour	2 or 4
Chicken thighs (bone in)	147°F (64°C)	1 hour, 30 minutes	8
	154°F (68°C)	1 hour	4
Chicken thighs (boneless)	154°F (68°C)	6 hours	2 lb. (1kg)
Chicken wings	150°F (66°C)	2 hours	12
Duck legs	170°F (77°C)	12 hours	2
Eggs	poached: 145°F (63°C); soft-boiled: 150°F (66°C); hard-boiled: 165°F (74°C)	1 hour	4 large
Turkey breasts	145°F (63°C)	4 hours	2
Whole chicken (cooked in 1 bag)	147°F (64°C)	3 hours	1, cut into 8 pieces and breastbones removed
Whole chicken (cooked in 2 bags)	thighs and legs (dark meat): 155°F (68°C) and 145°F (63°C)	2 hours	2 each
	breast halves and wings (white meat): 145°F (63°C)	1 hour	2 each
Whole chicken (cut into quarters)	147°F (64°C)	1 hour, 30 minutes	4 lb. (2kg)

When cooking eggs sous vide, **the shell acts as a natural seal.** All you need to do is preheat the water to the desired doneness and then slide the eggs into the water.

This hearty soup, with moist chunks of chicken, buttery egg noodles, and fresh veggies, retains healthy nutrients with the help of sous vide

CHICKEN NOODLE
soup

 2 hours, 50 minutes

 183°F (84°C) and 147°F (64°C)

 8 servings

½ red bell pepper, diced

¼ cup carrots, chopped

½ cup white onions, diced

½ cup yellow squash, diced

4 cups fresh baby spinach

½ tsp. garlic powder

½ tsp. onion powder

½ tsp. sea salt

½ tsp. ground black pepper

Dash cayenne pepper (optional)

1 TB. extra-virgin olive oil

2 (6-oz.; 170g) boneless and skinless chicken breasts, diced

2 qt. (2l) chicken broth

1 cup dried egg noodles

PREP AND SEAL 20 minutes

1 Preheat the sous vide machine to 183°F (84°C).

2 In a large bowl, combine red bell pepper, carrots, white onions, yellow squash, and baby spinach.

3 Add garlic powder, onion powder, sea salt, black pepper, cayenne pepper (if using), and extra virgin olive oil, and toss to season and coat.

4 Put seasoned vegetables in a 1-quart (1l) plastic bag and seal.

COOK 2 hours

1 Once the sous vide water bath has reached the desired temperature, insert the plastic bag of vegetables and allow to cook for 1 hour.

2 Remove the plastic bag from the water bath and place in the refrigerator to cool for 1 hour.

3 Meanwhile, reduce the temperature of the sous vide water bath to 147°F (64°C).

4 Put diced chicken breasts in a 1-quart (1l) plastic bag and seal.

5 Once the sous vide water bath has reached the desired temperature, insert the plastic bag of chicken and allow to cook for 1 hour. Set aside.

FINISH 30 minutes

1 In a large stockpot, pour chicken broth. Strain liquid from the plastic bags of seasoned vegetables and chicken and add to broth.

2 Bring liquid to a boil over high heat. Add egg noodles and allow to cook until al dente, about 8 minutes.

3 Add cooked vegetables and chicken to the pot and reduce heat to low. Return broth to a simmer and allow to cook for 5 minutes.

4 Remove soup from heat and serve immediately.

PREP AND SEAL   15 minutes

1 Preheat the sous vide machine to 150°F (66°C).

2 Season both sides of chicken breasts with Madras curry powder.

3 Put seasoned chicken breasts in a 1-quart (1l) plastic bag and seal.

COOK   1 hour

1 Once the sous vide water bath has reached the desired temperature, insert the plastic bag of chicken breasts and allow to cook for 1 hour.

2 Remove the plastic bag from the water bath and place in the refrigerator.

FINISH   2 hours, 15 minutes

1 Allow chicken breasts to cool until completely chilled, about 2 hours. Take out of the refrigerator and remove from the plastic bag, discarding liquid inside.

2 Dice chicken breasts into ½-inch (1.25cm) pieces.

3 In a large bowl, combine diced chicken, red grapes, walnut pieces, red curry powder, Worcestershire sauce, and extra-thick mayonnaise.

4 Serve chicken salad on salad greens or between two slices of your favorite bread.

Sweet red grapes balance an extra-hot dose of curry powder in this tasty chicken salad. Toasted walnuts add a satisfying crunch.

CURRIED CHICKEN
salad

 3 hours, 30 minutes

150°F (66°C)

4 servings

4 (4- to 6-oz.; 110 to 170g) boneless and skinless chicken breasts

4 TB. Madras curry powder or red curry powder of your choice

8 red grapes, cut in half

¼ cup walnut pieces, toasted

1 TB. red curry powder

¼ tsp. Worcestershire sauce

½ cup extra-thick mayonnaise

Curried chicken salad **originated in England as a dish served for the coronation of Queen Elizabeth II.** She had her cooks create this special chicken dish for a luncheon she hosted for foreign dignitaries at the time—hence it also being known as *coronation chicken.*

Fried chicken is a true comfort food when done right. Cooking it sous vide before crisping the skin in hot oil ensures your chicken stays moist and tender.

FRIED
chicken

 3 hours

 155°F (68°C) and 145°F (63°C)

4 servings

1 (2½-lb.; 1.15kg) whole chicken

½ tsp. garlic powder

¼ tsp. onion powder

½ tsp. smoked paprika

1 TB. dried tarragon

8 cups peanut oil

2 TB. kosher salt

1 cup buttermilk

2 cups all-purpose flour

| PREP AND SEAL | 20 minutes |

1 Preheat the sous vide machine to 155°F (68°C).

2 Using a sharp knife, cut whole chicken into 8 pieces: 2 breast halves, 2 thighs, 2 legs, and 2 wings. Remove bones from breast halves.

3 In a medium bowl, combine garlic powder, onion powder, smoked paprika, and tarragon. Season chicken pieces with spice mixture.

4 Put seasoned chicken breast halves and wings (white meat) in a 1-quart (1l) plastic bag and seal. Put seasoned chicken thighs and legs (dark meat) in a separate 1-quart (1l) plastic bag and seal.

| COOK | 2 hours, 10 minutes |

1 Once the sous vide water bath has reached the desired temperature, insert the plastic bag of chicken thighs and legs and allow to cook for 1 hour.

2 Reduce the sous vide water bath temperature to 145°F (63°C).

3 Leaving the plastic bag of chicken thighs and legs in the water, insert the plastic bag of chicken breast halves and wings into the water once the sous vide water bath has reached the desired temperature. Allow to cook for 1 hour. Remove both plastic bags from the water.

| FINISH | 30 minutes |

1 Allow the bags of chicken to cool for 10 minutes. In a large Dutch oven or other heavy pot, add peanut oil. Place on the stovetop and bring to a temperature of 400°F (204°C) over high heat.

2 Remove chicken pieces from both plastic bags and sprinkle with kosher salt.

3 Place buttermilk and all-purpose flour in two separate medium bowls.

4 Dredge chicken pieces first in flour, and then in buttermilk, and finally in flour again. Allow coated chicken to sit on a plate at room temperature for 15 minutes.

5 Once oil has reached the desired temperature, add coated chicken pieces to the Dutch oven and allow to cook until exterior is a golden brown color, about 2 minutes.

6 Remove fried chicken from oil, placing on paper towels, and allow to cool slightly before serving.

PREP AND SEAL   10 minutes

1 Preheat the sous vide machine to 147°F (64°C).

2 Dry chicken breasts with a paper towel.

3 Put chicken breasts in a 1-quart (1l) plastic bag and seal.

COOK   1 hour

1 Once the sous vide water bath has reached the desired temperature, insert the plastic bag of chicken breasts and allow to cook for 1 hour.

2 Remove chicken breasts from the plastic bag and dry again with paper towels. Set aside.

FINISH   1 hour, 5 minutes

1 In a large pot filled with cold water, soak rice noodles for 45 minutes.

2 Meanwhile, preheat a wok or large sauté pan on high.

3 In a medium bowl, combine tamarind paste, fish sauce, rice wine vinegar, and sugar. Set aside.

4 Cut chicken breasts into ¼-inch (.5cm) strips. In a medium bowl, toss chicken with kosher salt.

5 Once the wok has reached the desired temperature, add chicken strips and vegetable oil. Allow chicken to cook on one side until browned, about 30 seconds. Remove chicken from the wok and place on a cold plate.

6 Continuing to keep the wok hot, add garlic, shallot, and unsalted peanuts. Cook, quickly moving ingredients around the pan so they don't burn, for about 30 seconds or until lightly toasted.

7 Add vinegar-sugar mixture to the wok and allow to cook until liquid starts to steam. Immediately remove ingredients from the wok and pour over reserved chicken strips.

8 Sprinkle with chili pepper, bean sprouts, and white pepper.

9 When rice noodles are ready, drain. In a large bowl, toss noodles with seasoned chicken strips. Serve pad Thai with cilantro and lime wedges.

This dish features rice noodles and sous vide chicken tossed with crunchy peanuts, fragrant garlic, mild shallots, and a sweet and savory sauce.

PAD
thai

 2 hours, 15 minutes

 147°F (64°C)

 4 servings

4 (8-oz.; 225g) boneless and skinless chicken breasts

7 oz. (200g) rice noodles

⅓ cup tamarind paste

2 TB. fish sauce

2 TB. rice wine vinegar

2 TB. granulated sugar

1 tsp. kosher salt

2 TB. vegetable oil

1 TB. minced garlic

1 minced shallot

¼ cup unsalted peanuts

Pinch ground white pepper

¼ tsp. ground dried chili pepper

½ cup bean sprouts

2 TB. chopped fresh cilantro

4 lime wedges

In this recipe, chicken thighs are cooked sous vide and then refrigerated overnight before being smoked. The result is juicy meat with a mouthwatering smoke flavor.

SMOKED CHICKEN
thighs

 10 hours, 15 minutes

 147°F (64°C)

 4 servings

1 TB. paprika
1 TB. dark brown sugar, tightly packed
$^1/_2$ tsp. ground black pepper
$^1/_2$ tsp. garlic powder
$^1/_2$ tsp. dry mustard
$^1/_8$ tsp. cumin
$^1/_8$ tsp. cayenne pepper
8 (6-oz.; 170g) chicken thighs
1 TB. kosher salt
$^1/_2$ cup barbecue sauce

PREP AND SEAL   20 minutes

1 Preheat the sous vide machine to 147°F (64°C).

2 In a medium bowl, combine paprika, dark brown sugar, black pepper, garlic powder, dry mustard, cumin, and cayenne pepper.

3 Dry chicken thighs with a paper towel. Rub spice mixture onto chicken thighs.

4 Divide seasoned chicken thighs between two 1-gallon (3.75l) plastic bags and seal.

COOK   1 hour, 30 minutes

1 Once the sous vide water bath has reached the desired temperature, insert the plastic bags of chicken thighs and allow to cook for 1 hour, 30 minutes.

2 Remove the plastic bags from the water bath.

FINISH   8 hours, 25 minutes

1 Remove chicken thighs from the plastic bags and sprinkle with kosher salt. Place, uncovered, in the refrigerator overnight to cool.

2 Preheat a smoker to 200°F (93°C).

3 Remove chicken thighs from the refrigerator and dry with paper towels.

4 Place chicken thighs on the smoker and cook until an internal temperature of 150°F (66°C) is reached. Remove to a large plate.

5 Preheat a grill to medium-high heat.

6 Coat chicken thighs with barbecue sauce and place on the grill briefly to caramelize sugars in the sauce, about 2 to 3 minutes.

7 Remove chicken thighs from the grill and serve immediately.

This classic Burgundy dish–comprised of chicken, red wine, mushrooms, and garlic–has the alcohol boiled off to ensure even sous vide cooking.

COQ AU
vin

 4 hours, 55 minutes

 147°F (64°C)

 4 servings

3 TB. extra-virgin olive oil

1 (4-lb.; 2kg) whole chicken, cut into 8 pieces and breastbones removed

½ tsp. sea salt

2 white onions, diced

2 cups fresh white button mushrooms, sliced

2 large cloves garlic, minced

⅓ cup brandy (optional)

1 cups pinot noir

1 large ripe, red, and unpeeled tomato, chopped, or ⅓ cup canned Italian plum tomatoes

1 cup chicken stock

1 bay leaf

¼ tsp. thyme

Kosher salt

Ground black pepper

PREP AND SEAL · 1 hour, 50 minutes

1 Add extra-virgin olive oil to a large sauté pan and preheat on high.

2 Lightly season chicken pieces with sea salt.

3 Add chicken to the sauté pan and sear until heavily browned, about 3 minutes per side. Remove chicken and allow to cool for 15 minutes. Set aside.

4 In the same pan, sauté white onions, white button mushrooms, and garlic until mushrooms are dry, about 20 minutes.

5 Add brandy (if using) and pinot noir to deglaze the pan, stirring and scraping up browned bits at the bottom of the pan until they dissolve.

6 Allow wine-vegetable mixture to boil until the volume of liquid has reduced by half, about 15 minutes

7 Add tomato, chicken stock, bay leaf, and thyme. Allow to boil again until the new volume has reduced by half, about 15 minutes.

8 Remove the pan of liquid from the stovetop and chill to 70°F (21°C) in the refrigerator for 30 minutes.

9 Preheat the sous vide machine to 147°F (64°C).

10 Put chicken and liquid in a 1-gallon (3.75l) plastic bag and seal.

COOK · 3 hours

1 Once the sous vide water bath has reached the desired temperature, insert the plastic bag of chicken and liquid and allow to cook for 3 hours.

2 Remove the plastic bag from the water bath.

FINISH · 5 minutes

1 Remove chicken and liquid from the plastic bag, discarding bay leaf, and divide among plates.

2 Season chicken with kosher salt and black pepper to taste and serve.

Juicy and crisp chicken is paired with crunchy lettuce and cool, creamy Caesar dressing for a protein-filled salad you're sure to devour quickly.

CRISPY CHICKEN
caesar salad

 1 hour, 35 minutes

 147°F (64°C)

 2 servings

1 TB. Worcestershire sauce

1 tsp. mustard powder

1 tsp. ground black pepper

2 (6-oz.; 170g) boneless and skinless chicken breasts

3 cups peanut oil

1 TB. kosher salt

1/2 cup rice flour

2 oz. (55g) Romaine lettuce, cut into large strips

2 oz. (60ml) Caesar dressing

1/4 cup Parmesan cheese

PREP AND SEAL — 15 minutes

1 Preheat the sous vide machine to 147°F (64°C).

2 In a medium bowl, combine Worcestershire sauce, mustard powder, and black pepper.

3 Coat chicken breasts in sauce-seasoning mixture.

4 Put coated chicken breasts in a 1-quart (1l) plastic bag and seal.

COOK — 1 hour

1 Once the sous vide water bath has reached the desired temperature, insert the plastic bag of chicken and allow to cook for 1 hour.

2 Remove the plastic bag from the water bath and place in the refrigerator to cool.

FINISH — 20 minutes

1 In a large Dutch oven or other heavy pot, add peanut oil. Place on the stovetop and bring to a temperature of 350°F (177°C) over high heat.

2 Remove chicken breasts from the plastic bag and dry with paper towels.

3 Cut chicken breasts into 1/2-inch (1.25cm) strips and season with kosher salt.

4 Place rice flour in a medium bowl. Dredge chicken strips in rice flour to coat.

5 Once oil has reached the desired temperature, add coated chicken strips to the Dutch oven and allow to cook until exterior is a golden brown color, about 2 minutes. Remove chicken strips from oil and place on paper towels.

6 In a large bowl, toss the Romaine lettuce with Caesar dressing. Top with fried chicken strips and Parmesan cheese and serve.

These wings–cooked sous vide to ensure consistent doneness across the entire surface–are fried and then tossed in a fiery buffalo sauce.

BUFFALO CHICKEN
wings

 2 hours, 35 minutes

 150°F (66°C)

 4 servings

12 (5-oz.; 140g) chicken wings
1 tsp. smoked paprika
1 tsp. garlic powder
2 cups sunflower or vegetable oil
4 TB. kosher salt
1 tsp. cayenne pepper
2 cups rice flour
1 cup buffalo wing sauce

PREP AND SEAL   15 minutes

1 Preheat the sous vide machine to 150°F (66°C).

2 Season chicken wings with smoked paprika and garlic powder.

3 Put seasoned chicken wings in a 1-gallon (3.75l) plastic bag and seal.

COOK   2 hours

1 Once the sous vide water bath has reached the desired temperature, insert the plastic bag of chicken wings and allow to cook for 2 hours.

2 Remove chicken wings from the plastic bag and discard liquid inside the bag.

FINISH   20 minutes

1 In a large Dutch oven or other heavy pot, add sunflower oil. Place on the stovetop and bring to a temperature of 400°F (204°C) over high heat.

2 Season chicken wings with kosher salt and cayenne pepper.

3 Place rice flour in a medium bowl. Dredge chicken wings in rice flour. Allow coated chicken wings to sit for 15 minutes.

4 Once oil has reached the desired temperature, dredge chicken wings again and then add them to the Dutch oven. Allow chicken wings to cook on both sides until exterior is browned, about 2 minutes.

5 Remove chicken wings from oil and place in a large bowl. Add buffalo wing sauce and toss to coat. Serve immediately.

Savory chicken and sautéed onions are coated in a spicy teriyaki sauce and wrapped in butter lettuce leaves for a refreshing appetizer.

CHICKEN LETTUCE
wraps

 2 hours, 35 minutes

 145°F (63°C)

 4 servings

2 (8-oz.; 225g) boneless and skinless chicken breasts
2 cloves garlic, minced
1 TB. freshly grated ginger
1 head butter lettuce
$1/4$ cup hoisin sauce
2 TB. soy sauce
1 TB. rice wine vinegar
1 tsp. sriracha
1 TB. extra-virgin olive oil
1 white onion, diced
Kosher salt
Ground black pepper
1 green onion, thinly sliced

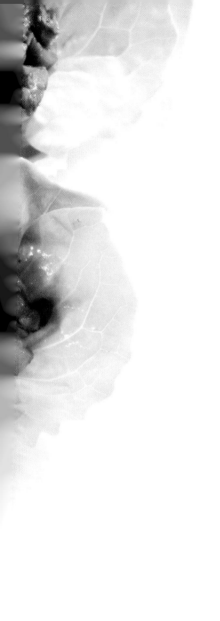

PREP AND SEAL   15 minutes

1 Preheat the sous vide machine to 145°F (63°C).

2 Dry chicken breasts with paper towels.

3 Put chicken breasts, garlic, and ginger in a 1-quart (1l) plastic bag and seal.

COOK   2 hours

1 Once the sous vide water bath has reached the desired temperature, insert the plastic bag of chicken with seasonings and allow to cook for 1 hour.

2 Remove the plastic bag from the water bath.

FINISH   20 minutes

1 Remove chicken breasts from the bag, discarding garlic and ginger, and chop into ¼-inch (.5cm) pieces. Place in a large bowl and set aside.

2 Separate butter lettuce into leaves. Place on a plate and set aside.

3 In a medium bowl, combine hoisin sauce, soy sauce, rice wine vinegar, and sriracha. Set aside.

4 In a large saucepan over high heat, sweat white onion pieces until translucent, about 1 to 2 minutes.

5 Add sauce mixture and cook until it starts to boil, about 1 minute.

6 Remove onion-sauce mixture from the saucepan and toss with chicken pieces.

7 Season chicken mixture with kosher salt and black pepper to taste.

8 Divide chicken mixture among lettuce leaves and serve with green onion slices and any leftover sauce on the side.

Traditionally, when making jerk chicken, **the chicken is smoked for hours over a fire of pimento and laurel woods.** For a more authentic version, add these woods to your grill in the final steps of cooking.

1 Preheat the sous vide machine to 147°F (64°C).

2 In a blender, place habanero pepper, red onion, vegetable oil, black pepper, allspice, cinnamon, nutmeg, and ginger and grind until smooth.

3 Dry chicken with paper towels. Pat spice blend onto chicken.

4 Put chicken in a 1-gallon (3.75l) plastic bag and seal.

COOK   1 hour, 30 minutes

1 Once the sous vide water bath has reached the desired temperature, insert the plastic bag of chicken and allow to cook for 1 hour, 30 minutes.

2 Remove the plastic bag from the water bath and set aside.

FINISH   30 minutes

1 Preheat a grill to high. In a medium bowl, combine malt vinegar, kosher salt, white rum, and molasses.

2 Remove chicken from the plastic bag and brush with rum-molasses glaze.

3 Once the grill has reached the desired temperature, place chicken skin side down on the grill and allow to cook until sugars on chicken caramelize, about 1 minute.

4 Turn chicken over and brush skin side with rum-molasses glaze.

5 Allow to cook until bone side of chicken has been caramelized, about 1 minute. Remove chicken from the grill.

6 Brush chicken with rum-molasses glaze one more time and serve.

This version of Jamaica's national dish cooks the chicken sous vide with a fiery-hot blend of peppers and spices and finishes it off with a rum-molasses glaze.

JERK
chicken

 2 hours, 10 minutes

 147°F (64°C)

 4 servings

1 habanero pepper, stemmed, seeded, and minced

1/2 red onion, chopped

1/4 cup vegetable oil

2 TB. ground black pepper

1/4 cup ground allspice

1 TB. ground cinnamon

1 tsp. ground nutmeg

1 TB. ground ginger

1 (4-lb.; 2kg) whole chicken, cut into quarters and breastbones removed

1/4 cup malt vinegar

1/4 cup kosher salt

1/4 cup white rum

1/2 cup molasses

Sweet, sour, and savory flavors are balanced at a high level in this dish, which combines juicy chicken with a mouthwatering teriyaki sauce.

TERIYAKI
chicken

 1 hour, 40 minutes

 154°F (68°C)

 4 servings

4 (4- to 6-oz.; 110 to 170g) skinless chicken thighs

2 cloves garlic clove, minced

1 TB. fresh ginger, minced

1 TB. soy sauce

2 TB. water

2 TB. sake

1 TB. light brown sugar, tightly packed

1 tsp. honey

1 cup uncooked white rice

2 cups chicken stock

PREP AND SEAL   10 minutes

1 Preheat the sous vide machine to 154°F (68°C).

2 Pat chicken thighs dry with paper towels.

3 Rub garlic and ginger into chicken thighs.

4 Put chicken in a 1-quart (1l) plastic bag and seal.

COOK   1 hour

1 Once the sous vide water bath has reached the desired temperature, insert the plastic bag of chicken thighs and allow to cook for 1 hour.

2 Remove the plastic bag from the water bath. Take chicken thighs out of the plastic bag.

FINISH   30 minutes

1 Shred chicken thighs, disposing of any bones. Set aside.

2 In a medium bowl, combine soy sauce, water, sake, light brown sugar, and honey to make teriyaki glaze. Set aside.

3 In a large stockpot, add white rice and chicken stock. Cook at medium-high heat until it comes to a simmer. Reduce heat to low, cover the pot, and cook for 15 minutes. Remove from heat and set aside.

4 Preheat a wok on high. Once the wok has reached the desired temperature, add shredded chicken and teriyaki glaze.

5 Immediately remove chicken with glaze from the wok when glaze starts to bubble, about 3 minutes.

6 Serve teriyaki chicken with cooked white rice.

Traditional turkey brings to mind large family gatherings. This recipe simply cooks turkey breast sous vide for a moist, manageable meal with few leftovers.

herbed
TURKEY BREAST

 4 hours, 50 minutes

 145°F (63°C)

 6 to 8 servings

2 (2-lb.; 1kg) pieces boneless turkey breast (from both sides of turkey)

1 TB. orange zest

1 TB. lemon zest

1 TB. fresh parsley, minced

1 tsp. ground black pepper

1 tsp. fresh thyme, minced

1 tsp. fresh rosemary, minced

1 tsp. garlic, minced

1 oz. (25g) cornstarch

1 pt. (.5l) chicken stock

2 TB. kosher salt

PREP AND SEAL   20 minutes

1 Preheat the sous vide machine to 145°F (63°C).

2 Dry turkey breast with paper towels.

3 In a medium bowl, combine orange zest, lemon zest, parsley, black pepper, thyme, rosemary, and garlic. Season turkey breast on both sides with mixture.

4 Put both pieces together skin side out and, using butcher's twine, tie together.

5 Put seasoned turkey breast in a 1-gallon (3.75l) plastic bag and seal.

COOK   4 hours

1 Once the sous vide water bath has reached the desired temperature, insert the plastic bag of seasoned turkey breast and allow to cook for 4 hours.

2 Remove the plastic bag from the water bath.

FINISH   30 minutes

1 Remove turkey breast from the bag, reserving liquid to make a gravy. Set aside.

2 In a medium stockpot, combine cornstarch and chicken stock.

3 Strain liquid from the bag through a fine-mesh sieve into chicken stock mixture.

4 Place gravy mixture on the stovetop and bring to a simmer over low heat to thicken. (Don't overcook, as cornstarch will lose its thickening power if it comes to a boil.) Season gravy to taste and set aside.

5 Remove the twine from turkey breast pieces. Dry pieces and season with kosher salt.

6 Brown skin of turkey breast pieces for 2 minutes, 30 seconds, in a hot saucepan over high heat or for about 1 minute with a blowtorch.

7 Slice turkey breast pieces and serve with gravy.

Made of shredded duck reserved in its own fat, duck rillettes can be spread onto bread and is oftentimes eaten with pickled vegetables.

DUCK
rillettes

 22 hours, 55 minutes

 170°F (77°C)

🍽 4 servings

2 (10-oz.; 285g) duck legs
3 sprigs fresh thyme
1 TB. kosher salt
1 tsp. ground black pepper
¼ tsp. dried bay leaves

PREP AND SEAL   8 hours, 10 minutes

1 Place duck legs, thyme, kosher salt, black pepper, and bay leaves in a 1-gallon (3.75l) plastic bag and seal.

2 Place the plastic bag in the refrigerator and allow meat to cure for 8 hours.

3 Preheat the sous vide machine to 170°F (77°C).

4 Remove duck legs from the plastic bag. Rinse off and dry with paper towels.

5 Place duck legs in a new 1-gallon (3.75l) plastic bag and seal.

COOK   12 hours

1 Once the sous vide water bath has reached the desired temperature, insert the plastic bag of duck legs and allow to cook for 12 hours.

2 Remove the plastic bag from the water bath.

FINISH   2 hours, 45 minutes

1 Place the plastic bag in an ice bath and allow to chill for 30 minutes.

2 Open the plastic bag and separate contents into three different bowls: duck, fat, and jellied liquid.

3 Remove skin and bones from duck and discard. In the bowl of a stand mixer with a paddle attachment, place duck meat and fat. Turn the mixer on low and allow to run for 1 minute.

4 Add ¼ cup of jellied liquid, discarding any extra. Turn the mixer on low and allow to run for 1 minute.

5 Scoop duck rillettes into four ramekins and store in the refrigerator until chilled, about 2 hours. Serve on slices of French bread or another bread of your choice. Rillettes can be stored in the refrigerator for up to 1 month.

Super easy and quick to throw together, these tacos include moist chicken, fresh lime juice, cool sour cream, and decadent queso.

SOUTHWEST CHICKEN
tacos

 7 hours, 20 minutes

 154°F (68°C)

 4 servings

2 lb. (1kg) boneless and skinless chicken thighs (about 6)

2 garlic cloves, thinly sliced

1/2 cup tomato salsa

1 TB. chopped canned chipotle peppers in adobo sauce

1 TB. chili powder

1 white onion, chopped

1/2 cup cilantro

Juice of 2 limes

1 cup queso fresco cheese

1/2 cup sour cream

16 fresh corn tortillas

PREP AND SEAL   10 minutes

1 Preheat the sous vide machine to 154°F (68°C).

2 Put chicken thighs, garlic, tomato salsa, chipotle peppers, and chili powder in a 1-gallon (3.75l) plastic bag and seal.

COOK   6 hours

1 Once the sous vide water bath has reached the desired temperature, insert the plastic bag of chicken thighs with seasonings and allow to cook for 6 hours.

2 Remove the plastic bag from the water bath.

FINISH   1 hour, 10 minutes

1 Remove chicken thighs from the bag and shred using two forks, discarding any bones. Set aside.

2 In a medium bowl, combine white onion, cilantro, and lime juice. Allow to marinate for at least 1 hour.

3 Layer shredded chicken, queso fresco cheese, marinated cilantro mixture, and sour cream on corn tortillas and serve.

Allow friends and family to customize their tacos by **providing different toppings and flavorings,** such as salsa, guacamole, lettuce, jalapeños, avocados, and lime juice.

Beef & Lamb

BEEF & LAMB
basics

Sous vide uses precision cooking, and nowhere is this more apparent than with beef and lamb. At a specific temperature for an exact period of time, the connective tissue will break down and disappear, leaving a moist meat with the proteins in place.

When it comes to beef, making the perfect steak may be the most-talked-about topic. The nice thing with sous vide is you don't have to invest a lot of money in a tender steak that can be grilled, broiled, or sautéed. Instead, you can buy tougher cuts and still get a tender, succulent meat that you can then finish as you'd like.

As for lamb, you get some of the best results when you cook it the sous vide way. Normally, you have to cook lamb at high temperatures in order to tenderize it. With sous vide, you can cook it at a lower temperature and get a tender meat that's also moist and full of flavor.

Because steaks often come in vacuum-sealed bags from the store, you have the option of leaving them in the bags instead of resealing them (as long as the bags are heat safe) for sous vide cooking. Not only will this save you a lot of time, you can still season the meat before you sear it to capture the perfect flavor.

Steak cooked sous vide

Steak cooked traditionally

When preparing...
Use herbs sparingly. With rosemary in particular, you'll find the flavor of herbs is intensified when sealed in with beef or lamb for sous vide cooking. This can lead to meat with an unpleasantly strong herbal taste. In most cases, you should use about a quarter of the amount that you would traditionally use in recipes.

When finishing...
Caramelize beef or lamb after cooking. The caramelization process allows the meat to develop a rich umami taste. Once you've removed the meat from the plastic bag, prepare it for caramelization by drying, salting, and oiling it. Finally, sear the beef or lamb using a skillet, grill, or blowtorch.

Rare

Medium Rare

Medium

BEEF & LAMB
times & temperatures

	COOKING TEMP	TIME	SIZE/NUMBER
Beef brisket	153°F (67°C)	36 hours	7 lb. (3kg)
	180°F (82°C)	10 hours	1 lb. (450g)
Beef chuck roast	179°F (82°C)	8 hours	1 lb. (450g) diced into 1-in. (2.5cm) chunks
Beef flank	134°F (57°C)	6 hours	1½ lb. (680g)
Beef knuckle	135°F (57°C)	48 hours	1 lb. (450g)
Beef shank	131°F (55°C)	48 hours	4 lb. (2kg)
Beef spare ribs	130°F (54°C)	72 hours	4 lb. (2kg)
	140°F (60°C)	48 hours	4 lb. (2kg)
Beef stew meat	149°F (65°C) to 150°F (66°C)	16 hours	1 lb. (450g) diced small to 2 lb. (1kg) cut into ½-in. (1.25cm) cubes
Ground beef	rare: 127°F (53°C)	1 hour	6 oz. (170g)
Lamb shoulder	133°F (56°C)	3 hours	1 lb. (450g) cut into a 1-in. (2.5cm) dice
	149°F (65°C)	16 hours	1 lb. (450g) cut into ½-in. (1.25cm) cubes
Rack of lamb	129°F (54°C)	1 hour	2 lb. (1kg); 8 bones
Rib-eye	medium rare: 133°F (56°C)	1 hour	1 in. (2.5cm) thick
Veal loin chop	140°F (60°C)	30 minutes	2

Medium Well

Well Done

PREP AND SEAL 15 minutes

1 Preheat the sous vide machine to 149°F (65°C).

2 Season lamb shoulder cubes with curry powder.

3 In a medium bowl, pour vegetable oil. Add seasoned lamb and toss.

4 Put seasoned lamb in a 1-quart (1l) plastic bag and seal.

COOK 16 hours

1 Once the sous vide water bath has reached the desired temperature, insert the plastic bag of seasoned lamb and allow to cook for 16 hours.

2 Remove the plastic bag from the water bath.

FINISH 45 minutes

1 Place the plastic bag in an ice bath and allow to chill for 15 minutes.

2 Open the plastic bag and separate contents into three different bowls: oil, lamb cubes, and broth.

3 In a large bowl, pour chicken stock. Strain broth from the bag and add to stock, stirring to combine.

4 In a large pot, add oil from the plastic bag and yellow onion and garlic. Cook over medium heat until onion is translucent, about 3 minutes.

5 Add ginger, almonds, coriander, cumin, turmeric, and cayenne pepper to the pot and toast until nice and fragrant, about 1 minute.

6 Whisk in chickpea flour until contents of the pot are evenly coated. Whisk in stock-broth mixture in a slow and steady stream and allow to cook for 2 minutes.

7 Bring soup to a simmer over high heat, whisking frequently, for 10 minutes.

8 Remove soup from the stovetop and add lamb cubes.

9 Ladle soup into bowls. Spoon ¼ cup white rice on each. Sprinkle with cilantro, salt, and black pepper to taste. Serve with lime wedges.

An English recipe inspired by Indian cuisine, this rich and spicy soup is served with rice for a hearty and complete meal.

MULLIGATAWNY
soup

 17 hours

 149°F (65°C)

 8 servings

1 lb. (450g) boneless lamb shoulder, cut into ¹/₂-in. (1.25cm) cubes

1¹/₂ tsp. curry powder

3 TB. vegetable oil

6 cups chicken stock

1 medium yellow onion, peeled and finely chopped

6 cloves garlic, peeled and finely chopped

1¹/₂ tsp. ginger, peeled and finely grated

1¹/₂ TB. almonds, toasted and ground into a fine powder

1¹/₂ tsp. ground coriander

1¹/₂ tsp. ground cumin

¹/₄ tsp. ground turmeric

¹/₂ tsp. cayenne pepper

¹/₄ cup chickpea flour

2 cups cooked white rice

Finely chopped fresh cilantro

Ground black pepper

Kosher salt

2 limes, quartered

This filling soup–packed with tender beef, a variety of vegetables, and flavorful barley–is a great cold-weather food.

BEEF BARLEY
soup

 17 hours, 30 minutes

 150°F (66°C) and 190°F (88°C)

 8 servings

2 lb. (1kg) beef stew meat, cut into ½-in. (1.25cm) cubes

½ tsp. ground black pepper

1 cup celery, diced

1 cup white onion, diced

1 TB. Worcestershire sauce

6 cups beef broth

⅔ cup barley

1 cup carrots, diced

3 TB. chopped tarragon

PREP AND SEAL   10 minutes

1 Preheat the sous vide machine to 150°F (66°C).

2 Put beef stew meat and black pepper in a 1-gallon (3.75l) plastic bag and seal.

COOK   17 hours

1 Once the sous vide water bath has reached the desired temperature, insert the plastic bag of seasoned beef and allow to cook for 16 hours.

2 Remove the plastic bag of seasoned beef and set aside. Increase the heat of the sous vide water bath to 190°F (88°C).

3 Put celery, white onion, Worcestershire sauce, beef broth, and barley in a 1-gallon (3.75l) plastic bag and seal.

4 Once the sous vide water bath has reached the desired temperature, insert the plastic bag of barley mixture and allow to cook for 1 hour.

FINISH   20 minutes

1 Place the contents of both bags into a large stockpot.

2 Add carrots and tarragon and bring to a simmer over high heat.

3 Immediately remove the pot of soup from the stovetop and serve.

This recipe is a perfect illustration of **how well grains cook sous vide.** While the broth cooks into the barley much like a pressure cooker, the barley won't become mushy. Also, because the barley is cooked separately from the beef, the beef will stay perfectly cooked while the barley cooks at a higher temperature.

Tender chunks of beef and seasonings are cooked together and then wrapped in warm tortillas for a truly filling taco.

BARBACOA
tacos

 8 hours, 35 minutes

 179°F (82°C)

 4 servings

1 lb. (450g) beef chuck roast, trimmed and diced into 1-in. (2.5cm) chunks

1 TB. ancho chile powder

1 TB. chopped chipotle peppers in adobo sauce

1 tsp. kosher salt

1/2 tsp. ground black pepper

16 corn tortillas

1 bunch cilantro, chopped

1 small yellow onion, thinly sliced

1 avocado, diced

2 limes, cut into wedges

PREP AND SEAL — 15 minutes

1 Preheat the sous vide machine to 179°F (82°C).

2 In a medium bowl, combine beef chunks, ancho chile powder, chipotle peppers, kosher salt, and black pepper.

3 Put seasoned beef in a 1-quart (1l) plastic bag and seal.

COOK — 8 hours

1 Once the sous vide water bath has reached the desired temperature, insert the plastic bag of seasoned beef and allow to cook for 8 hours.

2 Remove the plastic bag from the water bath.

FINISH — 20 minutes

1 Open the bag and place contents into a large bowl. Shred beef with a fork and set aside.

2 Warm corn tortillas in batches in the microwave for 10 seconds.

3 Top corn tortillas with shredded beef, cilantro, yellow onion, and avocado. Serve with lime wedges.

Beef chuck roast is a thick cut of meat from the shoulder of the cow. Because of this, it needs to be cooked for a long period of time in order for the meat to soften. Sous vide ensures you get that tender final product without losing any moisture from the meat.

Flank steak—a lean yet tough cut of meat—is cooked sous vide to produce a tender cut and grilled over high heat before being sliced into strips and served over a savory pesto pasta.

flank steak
WITH PESTO PASTA

 6 hours, 45 minutes

 134°F (57°C)

 4 servings

1$\frac{1}{2}$ lb. (680g) flank steak
1 tsp. ground black pepper
1 TB. kosher salt
2 TB. vegetable oil
6 cups cooked linguine
1$\frac{1}{2}$ cups pesto sauce

PREP AND SEAL   10 minutes

1 Preheat the sous vide machine to 134°F (57°C).

2 Season flank steak with black pepper.

3 Put seasoned steak in a 1-gallon (3.75l) plastic bag and seal.

COOK   6 hours

1 Once the sous vide water bath has reached the desired temperature, insert the plastic bag of seasoned steak and allow to cook for 6 hours.

2 Remove the plastic bag from the water bath.

FINISH   35 minutes

1 Preheat a grill to a temperature above 600°F (316°C). Meanwhile, allow steak to cool for 20 minutes.

2 Remove steak from the plastic bag and dry with paper towels.

3 Season steak with kosher salt. Rub vegetable oil onto steak.

4 Once the grill reaches the desired temperature, place steak on the grill and sear for 2 minutes per side.

5 Remove steak from the grill and allow to rest for 5 minutes.

6 Slice steak in ¼-inch (.5cm) strips across meat grain. Set aside.

7 In a large bowl, combine linguine and pesto sauce.

8 Divide pesto pasta among serving plates. Top with slices of steak and serve.

If you're one of those people looking for the perfect way to cook a steak, your search is over. This steak comes out right every time.

THE PERFECT
steak

 1 hour, 35 minutes

 133°F (56°C)

 1 serving

2 tsp. kosher salt

1/2 tsp. ground black pepper

1 clove garlic, minced

1 tsp. dried thyme

1 (16-oz.; 450g) rib-eye steak, cut 1 in. (2.5cm) thick

1 sprig rosemary

1 TB. vegetable oil

PREP AND SEAL — 10 minutes

1 Preheat the sous vide machine to 133°F (56°C).

2 In a medium bowl, combine kosher salt, black pepper, garlic, and thyme. Season rib-eye steak with mixture.

3 Put seasoned steak with rosemary in a 1-quart (1l) plastic bag and seal.

COOK — 1 hour

1 Once the sous vide water bath has reached the desired temperature, insert the plastic bag of seasoned steak and allow to cook for 1 hour for medium-rare doneness. (See the chart in the back of the book for other doneness levels.)

2 Remove the plastic bag from the water bath.

FINISH — 25 minutes

1 Preheat a grill to a temperature above 600°F (316°C).

2 Allow steak to rest for 10 minutes. Remove steak from the plastic bag and dry with paper towels.

3 Rub vegetable oil onto both sides of steak.

4 Once the grill reaches high heat, place steak on the grill and sear for 2 minutes per side.

5 Remove steak from the grill and allow to rest for 5 minutes. Serve.

PREP AND SEAL   15 minutes

1 Preheat the sous vide machine to 127°F (53°C).

2 Delicately form ground beef into a burger, taking care not to compress it too much.

3 Season hamburger with kosher salt and black pepper.

4 Put hamburger in a 1-quart (1l) zipper-lock bag and seal using the zipper-lock bag sealing method.

COOK   1 hour

1 Once the sous vide water bath has reached the desired temperature, insert the plastic bag of hamburger meat and allow to cook for 1 hour for rare doneness. (See the chart in the back of the book for other doneness levels.)

2 Remove the plastic bag from the water bath.

FINISH   20 minutes

1 Remove hamburger from the plastic bag and place on top of a paper towel. Allow to rest for 5 minutes.

2 Meanwhile, preheat a cast-iron skillet over medium-high heat until it starts smoking.

3 Rub vegetable oil onto both sides of hamburger.

4 Once the skillet reaches the desired temperature, place hamburger in it and sear on one side for about 2 minutes.

5 Flip hamburger and add cheddar cheese to top. Allow to sear for 2 minutes.

6 Remove cheeseburger from the skillet and serve on a toasted hamburger bun.

Because ground meat can become dry when compressed, this method doesn't involve vacuum sealing. The end result is a hamburger that's juicy and delicious.

THE ULTIMATE
cheese
burger

 1 hour, 35 minutes

 127°F (53°C)

 1 serving

6 oz. (170g) ground beef

1 tsp. kosher salt

$1/2$ tsp. ground black pepper

1 tsp. vegetable oil

2 slices cheddar cheese

1 toasted hamburger bun

Corned beef cooked traditionally can often be tough and dry. This sous vide corned beef–served with fragrant cabbage–is tender and moist, and will have you bragging to your friends.

corned beef
& CABBAGE

 19 hours

 180°F (82°C)

 1 serving

1 TB. kosher salt

⅛ tsp. pink salt (optional)

2 TB. pickling spice

1 lb. (450g) beef brisket

1 cup water

½ lb. (225g) carrots, peeled and roughly chopped

½ lb. (225g) russet potatoes, peeled

¼ head white or green cabbage, cut into 2 to 3 wedges

PREP AND SEAL   15 minutes

1 Preheat the sous vide machine to 180°F (82°C).

2 In a medium bowl, combine kosher salt, pink salt (if using), and pickling spice. Season beef brisket evenly on all sides with mixture.

3 Put seasoned beef brisket in a 1-gallon (3.75l) plastic bag and seal.

COOK   10 hours

1 Once the sous vide water bath has reached the desired temperature, insert the plastic bag of seasoned beef brisket and allow to cook for 10 hours.

2 Remove the plastic bag from the water bath.

FINISH   8 hours, 45 minutes

1 Place the plastic bag in the refrigerator and allow to cool overnight.

2 Remove corned beef from the plastic bag, scraping any gelatin off into the bag. Slice beef and fan out in a medium skillet. Set aside.

3 Put gelatinous liquid from the bag in a medium stockpot. Add water, carrots, russet potatoes, and cabbage.

4 Add ½ cup of liquid from the pot to the skillet with beef and place the skillet on top of the pot.

5 Cover the skillet with a lid of aluminum foil. Bring the pot underneath the skillet to a boil over high heat. Reduce to a simmer and cook until vegetables are tender and beef is heated through, about 30 minutes.

6 Place corned beef and cabbage on a plate. Separate cooked carrots, cooked potatoes, and liquid into separate bowls. Serve immediately.

This recipe uses a tougher cut of meat from the top round of beef called a *knuckle*. Because it's typically ground, you'll need to **ask your local butcher for the cut of meat.** By cooking beef knuckle at a low temperature for 48 hours, you'll make this meat much more delicate and flavorful.

PREP AND SEAL   15 minutes

1 Preheat the sous vide machine to 135°F (57°C).

2 Season beef knuckle with kosher salt and black pepper.

3 Put seasoned beef knuckle in a 1-quart (1l) plastic bag and seal.

COOK   48 hours

1 Once the sous vide water bath has reached the desired temperature, insert the plastic bag of seasoned beef and allow to cook for 48 hours.

2 Remove the plastic bag from the water bath.

FINISH   8 hours, 20 minutes

1 Place in the bag the refrigerator to chill overnight. Once chilled, preheat a cast-iron skillet over high heat.

2 Meanwhile, remove beef knuckle from the plastic bag and slice into paper-thin pieces.

3 Once the skillet reaches the desired temperature, add vegetable oil.

4 Place beef slices in the skillet and cook until a dark brown color, about 1 minute. Remove from the skillet and set aside.

5 In the still-hot skillet, place white onions. Allow to cook until onions are completely browned and caramelized, about 1 minute. Remove onions from the skillet and set aside.

6 Spread 4 tablespoons Cheez Whiz on each hoagie roll.

7 Layer rolls with cooked beef and onions and serve.

This nod to the Philadelphia staple combines the rich flavor of beef, the caramelized sweetness of onion, and the tang of cheese.

PHILLY
cheese steak

 56 hours, 35 minutes

 135°F (57°C)

 4 servings

1 lb. (450g) beef knuckle

2 tsp. kosher salt

½ tsp. ground black pepper

4 TB. vegetable oil

2 medium white onions, peeled and diced

1 cup Cheez Whiz or other processed cheese spread

4 soft hoagie rolls

Beef shank is tenderized by the sous vide process and then coated in a rich sauce for a dish that's savory and moist.

BEEF OSSO
buco

 48 hours, 45 minutes

 131°F (55°C)

 4 servings

4 lb. (2kg) beef shank
¼ cup all-purpose flour
4 TB. vegetable oil
2 tsp. kosher salt
½ tsp. ground black pepper

PREP AND SEAL　　　　　　　15 minutes

1 Preheat the sous vide machine to 131°F (55°C).

2 Season beef shank with kosher salt and black pepper.

3 Put seasoned beef shank in a 1-gallon (3.75l) plastic bag and seal.

COOK　　　　　　　　　　48 hours

1 Once the sous vide water bath has reached the desired temperature, insert the plastic bag of seasoned beef shank and allow to cook for 48 hours.

2 Remove the plastic bag from the water bath.

FINISH　　　　　　　　　30 minutes

1 Open the plastic bag and pour liquid from it into a container to reserve. Place beef shank onto a cooling rack over a sheet pan.

2 In a medium saucepan over medium-high heat, place all-purpose flour and cook until it starts to toast and develops the aroma of popcorn, about 4 minutes.

3 Add vegetable oil and whisk with flour until all lumps are gone and oil-flour mixture (known as a *roux*) begins to foam, about 3 to 5 minutes.

4 Slowly pour reserved liquid from the plastic bag into roux, whisking vigorously as you do so. Reduce heat to low and allow sauce to simmer for 10 minutes.

5 Sear beef shank using your method of choice (a blowtorch, cast-iron skillet, or broiler).

6 Remove beef shank meat from the bone. Season with kosher salt and black pepper.

7 Pour sauce onto a plate, place beef shank on top, and serve.

These ribs, cut in strips through the bone (also known as *flanken*), are marinated and fried before being covered in a sweet and tangy sauce.

KOREAN-STYLE
short
ribs

 48 hours, 45 minutes

 140°F (60°C)

 4 servings

2¹/₂ cups filtered water
²/₃ cup tamari (gluten-free soy sauce)
¹/₄ cup apple juice
3 TB. mirin
1 TB. sesame oil
1 Asian pear, peeled, cored, and chopped
1 medium yellow onion
1 tsp. ground white pepper
4 lb. (2kg) beef spare ribs
¹/₄ cup vegetable oil

PREP AND SEAL

20 minutes

1. Preheat the sous vide machine to 140°F (60°C).

2. In a blender, place filtered water, tamari, apple juice, mirin, sesame oil, Asian pear, yellow onion, and white pepper. Blend on high until the consistency of a marinade.

3. Put beef spare ribs and marinade in a 1-gallon (3.75l) plastic bag and seal.

COOK

48 hours

1. Once the sous vide water bath has reached the desired temperature, insert the plastic bag of spare ribs and allow to cook for 48 hours.

2. Remove the plastic bag from the water bath.

FINISH

25 minutes

1. Remove spare ribs from the plastic bag and set aside. Strain liquid from the plastic bag through a fine-mesh sieve into a large saucepan.

2. On a stovetop over high heat, cook sauce until the volume is reduced to 2 cups, about 5 minutes. Remove the saucepan from heat and set aside.

3. In a large stockpot, add vegetable oil. Place on the stovetop and preheat to medium-high.

4. Remove bones and trim any excessive fat from spare ribs.

5. Once oil has reached the desired temperature, add spare ribs and fry until they turn a deep mahogany color, about 8 minutes.

6. Remove short ribs from oil, coat with sauce, and serve immediately on its own or paired with kimchi.

This soup really showcases the good qualities of sous vide cooking. The vegetables keep their shape and the tough meat softens, creating a rich, flavorful final product.

BEEF VEGETABLE
soup

 17 hours, 50 minutes

 149°F (65°C) and 185°F (85°C)

 8 servings

1 lb. (450g) beef stew meat, diced small

1 tsp. garlic powder

1 cup white onion, diced small

1/2 cup celery, diced small

1/2 cup carrots, diced small

1 russet potato, diced small

2 TB. extra-virgin olive oil

3 1/2 cups beef broth

1/2 cup frozen corn

1/2 cup frozen peas

1 (14-oz.; 400g) can diced tomatoes

1 small bay leaf

2 tsp. hot sauce

Kosher salt

Ground black pepper

PREP AND SEAL — 20 minutes

1 Preheat the sous vide machine to 149°F (65°C).

2 Put vegetables in a 1-quart (1l) plastic bag and seal.

3 Season beef stew meat with garlic powder.

4 Put seasoned beef in a 1-quart (1l) plastic bag and seal.

COOK — 17 hours

1 Once the sous vide water bath has reached the desired temperature, insert the plastic bag of seasoned meat and allow to cook for 16 hours.

2 Remove the plastic bag from the water bath and place in the refrigerator.

3 Increase the temperature of the sous vide water bath to 185°F (85°C).

4 In a large bowl, combine white onion, celery, carrots, and potato. Add extra-virgin olive oil and toss.

5 Put vegetables in a 1-quart (1l) plastic bag and seal.

6 Once the sous vide water bath has reached the desired temperature, insert the plastic bag of vegetables and allow to cook for 1 hour. Remove the plastic bag from the water bath.

FINISH — 30 minutes

1 In a large stockpot, pour beef broth. Open both plastic bags and strain liquid into beef broth using a fine-mesh sieve.

2 Bring beef broth to a boil over high heat. Add corn, peas, tomatoes, and bay leaf, and simmer over medium-high heat.

3 Add cooked vegetables and seasoned beef to the pot. Return broth to a simmer. Once it reaches a simmer, remove from heat immediately.

4 Remove bay leaf. Season soup with hot sauce, as well as kosher salt and black pepper to taste. Serve.

This recipe captures the delicate balance between meat falling apart and being tough, and combines it with liquid smoke and spices for a perfectly seasoned brisket.

SMOKED
brisket

 37 hours, 5 minutes

153°F (67°C)

10 servings

2 TB. kosher salt

2 TB. light brown sugar, tightly packed

1 TB. ground black pepper

2 tsp. cayenne pepper

1 TB. paprika

2 tsp. thyme leaves

2 tsp. ground cumin

1 tsp. granulated garlic

7 lb. (3kg) beef brisket

$1/4$ tsp. Prague powder #1

1 tsp. liquid smoke

PREP AND SEAL — 20 minutes

1 Preheat the sous vide machine to 153°F (67°C).

2 In a medium bowl, combine kosher salt, light brown sugar, black pepper, cayenne pepper, paprika, thyme, cumin, and garlic, making sure to disperse herbs and spices. Divide rub into two equal portions. Set aside.

3 Trim thickest areas of fat off beef brisket, leaving a fat layer ¼ inch (.5cm) thick.

4 Using half of rub, season both sides of beef brisket.

5 Sprinkle Prague powder #1 and liquid smoke onto both sides of beef brisket.

6 Put seasoned beef brisket in a 1-gallon (3.75l) plastic bag and seal.

COOK — 36 hours

1 Once the sous vide water bath has reached the desired temperature, insert the plastic bag of beef brisket and allow to cook for 36 hours.

2 Remove the plastic bag from the water bath.

FINISH — 45 minutes

1 Preheat an oven to 350°F (177°C).

2 Remove beef brisket from the plastic bag and dry meat with paper towels.

3 Season beef brisket with remaining half of rub. Place on a sheet pan with a wire rack.

4 When the oven has reached the desired temperature, insert the sheet pan and bake beef brisket for 15 minutes to set bark crust on outside of brisket.

5 Remove beef brisket from the oven and allow to rest for 15 minutes.

6 Slice beef brisket into $1/3$-inch (.75cm) slices before serving.

Beef spare ribs are usually braised for long periods of time, leading to a flaky texture. In this recipe, the spare ribs are tenderized with sous vide and then finished more like a steak.

BEEF SPARE
ribs

 72 hours, 45 minutes

 130°F (54°C)

 4 servings

1 TB. kosher salt

1 tsp. granulated sugar

1 tsp. ground black pepper

1/2 tsp. fresh rosemary leaves, chopped

4 lb. (2kg) beef spare ribs

PREP AND SEAL — 20 minutes

1 Preheat the sous vide machine to 130°F (54°C).

2 In a small bowl, combine kosher salt, sugar, black pepper, and rosemary. Set aside.

3 Trim away any large pieces of fat from beef spare ribs.

4 Using seasoning mixture, season spare ribs evenly on all sides.

5 Put seasoned spare ribs in two 1-gallon (3.75l) plastic bags and seal.

COOK — 72 hours

1 Once the sous vide water bath has reached the desired temperature, insert the plastic bag of spare ribs and allow to cook for 72 hours.

2 Remove the plastic bag from the water bath.

FINISH — 25 minutes

1 Remove spare ribs from the plastic bag and dry meat with paper towels.

2 Strain liquid from the plastic bag through a fine-mesh sieve into a large saucepan.

3 On the stovetop over high heat, cook liquid until it reduces to a glaze, about 10 minutes. Set aside.

4 Remove bone from spare ribs. Sear spare ribs with a blowtorch, in a cast-iron skillet, or on a hot grill for about 1 minute per side.

5 Coat spare ribs in glaze and serve.

This tender cut of meat is cooked similarly to a beef cut and is paired with a creamy, mushroom-flavored béchamel sauce.

veal chop
WITH WILD MUSHROOM BÉCHAMEL SAUCE

 1 hour

 140°F (60°C)

2 servings

1 tsp. kosher salt

1/8 tsp. ground white pepper

1/2 tsp. fresh tarragon leaves, chopped

2 (10-oz.; 285g) veal loin chops

8 oz. (237ml) mushroom cream (see Infusions)

4 TB. vegetable oil

2 TB. all-purpose flour

PREP AND SEAL — 10 minutes

1 Preheat the sous vide machine to 140°F (60°C).

2 In a small bowl, combine kosher salt, white pepper, and tarragon.

3 Season veal loin chops evenly on both sides with mixture.

4 Put seasoned veal chops in a 1-gallon (3.75l) plastic bag and seal.

COOK — 30 minutes

1 Once the sous vide water bath has reached the desired temperature, insert the plastic bag of veal chops and allow to cook for 30 minutes.

2 Remove the plastic bag from the water bath.

FINISH — 20 minutes

1 Remove veal chops from the plastic bag and dry with paper towels.

2 In a large bowl, pour mushroom-infused heavy cream. Strain liquid from the plastic bag through a fine-mesh sieve into the bowl and stir. Set aside.

3 Preheat a cast-iron skillet over medium-high heat until it smokes heavily. Add vegetable oil followed immediately by veal chops and sear for about 2 to 3 minutes per side.

4 Remove veal chops from the skillet and set aside.

5 In the still-hot skillet, add all-purpose flour. Reduce heat to low and whisk with leftover oil for about 1 minute.

6 Whisk in cream mixture and simmer until béchamel reduces to 4 ounces (120ml), about 10 minutes.

7 Remove béchamel from heat and spoon onto plates. Place a veal chop on each plate and serve.

Mint sauce is often served with lamb, as the bitter taste goes well with the meat's flavor. This recipe tops sous vide-cooked and seared lamb with a mint-infused butter.

rack of lamb
WITH MINT-INFUSED BUTTER

 1 hour, 25 minutes

 129°F (54°C)

 2 servings

1 tsp. kosher salt
1/8 tsp. ground black pepper
1/2 tsp. fresh rosemary leaves, chopped
1 (2-lb.; 1kg) rack of lamb (8 bones)
1 tsp. Worcestershire sauce
2 TB. vegetable oil
1 oz. (25ml) mint butter (see Infusions)

PREP AND SEAL   **10 minutes**

1 Preheat the sous vide machine to 129°F (54°C).

2 In a small bowl, combine kosher salt, black pepper, and rosemary.

3 Season lamb evenly on both sides with mixture.

4 Put seasoned lamb and Worcestershire sauce in a 1-gallon (3.75l) plastic bag and seal.

COOK   **1 hour**

1 Once the sous vide water bath has reached the desired temperature, insert the plastic bag of lamb and allow to cook for 1 hour.

2 Remove the plastic bag from the water bath.

FINISH   **15 minutes**

1 Remove lamb from the plastic bag and dry meat with paper towels.

2 Cut lamb into four sections of two bones.

3 Add vegetable oil to a cast-iron skillet and preheat over high heat until it begins to smoke.

4 Add lamb pieces and sear for about 30 seconds per side. Remove lamb from the skillet.

5 Place two sections on each plate. Top each with mint butter and serve.

1 Preheat the sous vide machine to 133°F (56°C).

2 In a medium bowl, combine ginger, garlic, garam masala, cayenne pepper, kosher salt, and dried lemon peel. Season lamb shoulder pieces evenly on all sides with mixture.

3 Put seasoned lamb shoulder in a 1-gallon (3.75l) plastic bag and seal, making sure pieces are in a single layer.

Succulent lamb pieces are skewered and served with a cool mint yogurt sauce. Cooking the lamb sous vide before searing gives you the moistest, most flavorful meat.

LAMB TIKKA
kebabs

COOK   1 hour

1 Once the sous vide water bath has reached the desired temperature, insert the plastic bag of seasoned lamb shoulder and allow to cook for 3 hours.

2 Remove the plastic bag from the water bath.

 1 hour, 35 minutes

 133°F (56°C)

 4 servings

FINISH   20 minutes

1 Remove lamb shoulder pieces from the plastic bag and dry with paper towels.

2 Skewer lamb shoulder pieces on four wooden skewers.

3 Sear lamb kebabs for 2 minutes per side on a very hot grill or with a blowtorch until browned. Set aside.

4 In a medium bowl, combine mint leaves and Greek-style yogurt. Serve mint yogurt sauce alongside lamb kebabs.

1 tsp. powdered ginger
1 tsp. granulated garlic
1 tsp ground garam masala
¼ tsp. cayenne pepper
1 TB. kosher salt
1 TB. dried lemon peel
1 lb. (450g) lamb shoulder, cut into a 1-in. (2.5cm) dice
10 mint leaves, chopped
1 cup Greek-style yogurt

Make this a true Indian feast by spreading the mint yogurt sauce on a piece of naan bread, placing lamb from one skewer on top of the sauce, and rolling up the bread.

Pork

PORK
basics

Before the mid-twentieth century, pork fat was the most expensive part of the pig. However, once other cooking fats became prevalent on the market, the pork industry began breeding pigs to make them leaner.

This change in animal genetics means older pork recipes no longer work, as "rendering the fat" is no longer possible—there isn't any fat! And when it comes to tougher cuts, such as shoulder roasts, they need to be cooked over a long period of time in order to melt down the fibers that make the meat tough. Cooked the traditional way, a lean, tough cut of pork is more likely to come out dry and bland.

Cooking pork sous vide can help mitigate the loss of fat in pork by retaining moisture. This moisture, cooked at lower temperatures, can also help to break down the tough connective tissues. With the longer cooking times associated with sous vide, the connective tissue is given plenty of time to melt away, giving you a tenderer cut of meat. With all that moisture and tenderizing, you'll find your pork comes out with an amazing texture and rich flavor.

Pork cooked sous vide

Pork cooked traditionally

When preparing...
Sometimes pork needs is a bit of seasoning. A sprinkling of salt and pepper or a mixture of spices can enhance the meat's flavor during the sous vide process. Adding an acidic liquid (such as apple cider) to the sous vide bag helps complement the pork's sweetness, increasing the depth of flavor.

When finishing...
The flavor and the look of pork are more appreciable if it's smoked after making the meat tender via the sous vide process. First, give pork a bit of time to cool the food down. Once that's done, put it into a smoker for a few minutes. This extra finishing time is worth the enhanced smell and flavor.

PORK
times & temperatures

	COOKING TEMP	TIME	SIZE/NUMBER
Country pork ribs	150°F (66°C)	36 hours	1 rack
Ground pork	150°F (66°C)	1 hour	1½ lb. (680g)
Ham hock	132°F (56°C)	72 hours	1
Italian sausage	140°F (60°C)	1 hour	8 links
Pork belly	164°F (73°C)	6 hours	2 lb. (1kg)
Pork butt	158°F (70°C)	24 hours	1 lb. (450g), cut into 2-in. (5cm) cubes
Pork chops	medium rare: 140°F (60°C)	45 minutes	2 ¾- to 1-in.-thick (2 to 2.5cm)
	medium: 145°F (63°C)	1 hour	4 ½-in.-thick (1.25cm)
Pork roast	136°F (58°C)	5 hours	2 lb. (1kg)
Whole pork cheeks	158°F (70°C)	72 hours	2
Whole tenderloin	medium rare: 140°F (60°C)	1 hour	1

As with chicken, people are sometimes uneasy about eating pork with any pink color in the middle. While cooking pork sous vide for the prescribed times kills bacteria, **if you know your guests may not like the pink color,** cook the tender cuts of meat to 150°F (66°C) for the last 15 minutes to diminish the pinkish color.

A variation of the French *pot-au-feu* soup, this Vietnamese street food is a noodle soup with a rich broth, multiple types of meat, and various spices.

pho

 30 hours, 30 minutes

 136°F (58°C)

 8 servings

2 lb. (1kg) beef knuckle
2 lb. (1kg) beef brisket
1 white onion, charred
1 (4-in.; 10cm) piece ginger, charred
5 star anise pods
6 whole cloves
1 (3-in.; 7.5cm) piece cinnamon
2 lb. (1kg) pork roast
1 TB. kosher salt
1 TB. granulated sugar
1 tsp. soy sauce
1 TB. mirin
4 TB. fish sauce
2 TB. light brown sugar, tightly packed
1½ lb. (680g) rice noodles, soaked
20 mint leaves
20 basil leaves
20 cilantro leaves
½ lb. (225g) bean sprouts
8 lime wedges
2 TB. red chile sauce

PREP AND SEAL — 24 hours, 15 minutes

1 Preheat the sous vide machine to 136°F (58°C).

2 Combine beef knuckle, beef brisket, white onion, ginger, star anise pods, cloves, cinnamon, and enough water to cover. Use the sous vide technique for cooking broths (see Broths) for these ingredients. Cover and store in the refrigerator.

3 Season pork roast with kosher salt and sugar.

4 Put seasoned pork, soy sauce, and mirin in a 1-quart (1l) plastic bag and seal.

COOK — 5 hours

1 Once the sous vide water bath has reached the desired temperature, insert the plastic bag of pork and allow to cook for 5 hours.

2 Remove the plastic bag from the water bath and set aside.

FINISH — 1 hour, 15 minutes

1 Strain broth and measure the amount of broth and oil. Pour into a large stockpot and add enough water to bring the volume up to 10 cups.

2 Place the pot on the stovetop and bring broth and oil to a boil over high heat. Add fish sauce and light brown sugar, and keep broth at a slow rolling boil over medium-low heat for 1 hour.

3 Remove pork from the plastic bag, discarding liquid, and slice into 24 ¼-inch (.5cm) slices.

4 Divide rice noodles among bowls. Top noodles with three slices pork roast, and pour boiling broth over pork and noodles.

5 Serve pho with mint, basil, cilantro, bean sprouts, lime wedges, and red chile sauce on the side.

This recipe is a delightful treat for your taste buds, with sweet pork, acidic apples, spicy arugula, and bitter bleu cheese.

pork
& APPLE SALAD

 1 hour, 45 minutes

 145°F (63°C)

 4 servings

4 (8-oz.; 225g) ½-in.-thick (1.25cm) boneless pork chops

1 TB. kosher salt

½ tsp. ground black pepper

1 cup apple cider

2 tart apples, cored and medium dice

¼ cup poppy seed dressing

1 cup baby arugula, washed

2 oz. (55g) bleu cheese, crumbled

PREP AND SEAL — 15 minutes

1 Preheat the sous vide machine to 145°F (63°C).

2 Season pork chops with kosher salt and black pepper.

3 Put pork chops and apple cider in a 1-gallon (3.75l) plastic bag, making sure pork is in a single layer in the bag, and seal

COOK — 1 hour

1 Once the sous vide water bath has reached the desired temperature, insert the plastic bag of pork chops and apple cider and allow to cook for 1 hour for medium doneness. (See the chart in the back of the book for other doneness levels.)

2 Remove the plastic bag from the water bath.

FINISH — 30 minutes

1 Remove pork chops from the plastic bag, discarding liquid, and dry meat with paper towels.

2 Sear pork chops using a hot grill, cast-iron skillet, or blowtorch for 1 to 2 minutes per side. Set aside.

3 In a large bowl, place apples and poppy seed dressing and toss.

4 Separate baby arugula among bowls. Arrange apple mixture on top of arugula. Sprinkle bleu cheese crumbles, top with pork, and serve.

Searing the pork chops after cooking them sous vide adds a rich umami taste. A combination of sweet, salty, sour, and bitter, **umami helps balance out the flavors from other ingredients,** giving you a well-rounded dish full of flavor.

In this recipe, sous vide softens the beans and cooks out the chemicals that don't digest well. When combined with ham hock, this makes for a hearty comfort food.

HAM & BEAN
soup

 74 hours

 132°F (56°C) and 194°F (90°C)

 12 servings

1 (1-lb.; 450g) ham hock
1 lb. (450g) navy beans
2 qt. (2l) water
1 tsp. kosher salt
1 white onion, chopped
Ground black pepper (optional)

PREP AND SEAL — 15 minutes

1 Preheat the sous vide machine to 132°F (56°C).

2 Put ham hock in a 1-quart (1l) plastic bag and seal.

COOK — 73 hours, 30 minutes

1 Once the sous vide water bath has reached the desired temperature, insert the plastic bag of ham hock and allow to cook for 72 hours.

2 Remove the plastic bag from the water bath and store in the refrigerator until needed.

3 In a large stockpot, place navy beans and 5 cups water. Allow to soak overnight.

4 Preheat the sous vide machine to 194°F (90°C).

5 Drain water off navy beans. Combine navy beans, kosher salt, white onion, and remaining 3 cups water in a 1-gallon (3.75l) plastic bag and seal.

6 Once the sous vide water bath has reached the desired temperature, insert the plastic bag of bean soup and allow to cook for 1 hour, 30 minutes.

7 Squeeze a bean inside the plastic bag to see whether it's tender and remove from the water bath if that's the case. (If it isn't, cook in 15-minute intervals until beans are cooked through.)

FINISH — 15 minutes

1 Remove ham hock from the plastic bag, discarding liquid.

2 Cut off ham hock skin and then shred meat.

3 In a large bowl, pour in bean soup and add shredded ham hock. Season to taste with kosher salt and black pepper, if you'd like, and serve.

This hearty salad includes pork meatballs flavored with traditional Thai spices. The meatballs are coated with a spicy-sweet dressing and served over lettuce.

THAI PORK MEATBALL
salad

 1 hour, 50 minutes

 150°F (66°C)

 8 servings

2 lemongrass stalks, tender inner part, bottom 4 in. (10cm) only

3 shallots, peeled

¼ cup fresh cilantro

3 green onions

1 (1-in.; 2.5cm) piece ginger, peeled

1 small jalapeño, stemmed and seeded

2 TB. + ¼ cup fish sauce

1 tsp. coarse salt

1½ lb. (680g) ground pork

¼ cup lime juice

3 TB. vegetable oil

2 TB. granulated sugar

2 TB. grated carrot

2 TB. grated cucumber

3 TB. sambal oelek chile sauce

1 head Bibb lettuce

2 cucumbers, julienned

PREP AND SEAL — 30 minutes

1 Preheat the sous vide machine to 150°F (66°C).

2 In a food processor, place lemongrass, shallots, cilantro, green onions, ginger, jalapeño, 2 tablespoons fish sauce, and coarse salt. Pulse until mixture is chopped into fine pieces.

3 In a stand mixer fitted with a paddle attachment, combine chopped mixture and ground pork on low speed until mixture is evenly distributed. (Don't overmix, as this will result in meatballs that are dry and firm.)

4 Form seasoned meat into 40 ½-inch (1.25cm) meatballs.

5 Put meatballs in a 1-gallon (3.75l) plastic bag and seal.

COOK — 1 hour

1 Once the sous vide water bath has reached the desired temperature, insert the plastic bag of meatballs and allow to cook for 1 hour.

2 Remove the plastic bag from the water bath and set aside.

FINISH — 20 minutes

1 In a medium bowl, combine lime juice, remaining ¼ cup fish sauce, vegetable oil, sugar, carrot, grated cucumber, and sambal oelek chile sauce.

2 Remove meatballs from the plastic bag. Add to dressing and toss to coat.

3 Divide Bibb lettuce and then julienned cucumber among plates. Top each with meatballs and serve.

PREP AND SEAL — 20 minutes

1 Preheat the sous vide machine to 140°F (60°C).

2 Season pork chops with kosher salt and black pepper.

3 Put seasoned pork chops and sour cherry juice in a 1-gallon (3.75l) plastic bag and seal.

COOK — 45 minutes

1 Once the sous vide water bath has reached the desired temperature, insert the plastic bag of pork chops and allow to cook for 45 minutes for medium-rare doness. (See the chart in the back of the book for other doneness levels.)

2 Remove the plastic bag from the water bath.

FINISH — 30 minutes

1 Remove pork chops and juice from the bag, separating meat from juice. Strain juice through a fine-mesh sieve into a medium bowl and set aside.

2 Dry pork chops with paper towels. Coat dried pork chops in vegetable oil.

3 In a cast-iron skillet over high heat, sear both sides of oiled pork chops, about 1 to 2 minutes per side.

4 Remove seared pork chops from the skillet, place each on a plate, and set aside.

5 Deglaze the still-hot skillet with pinot noir wine. Add strained juices and cook until liquid is reduced down to a syrup consistency, about 5 minutes.

6 Pour glaze over pork chops and serve.

These pork chops, cooked sous vide to the specifications of a steak of medium doneness, are served in a tart cherry glaze.

pork chops
WITH CHERRY GLAZE

 1 hour, 35 minutes

 140°F (60°C)

 2 servings

2 (12-oz.; 340g) ¾- to 1-in.-thick (2 to 2.5cm) boneless pork chops

1 TB. kosher salt

1 tsp. ground black pepper

2 TB. sour cherry juice

1 TB. vegetable oil

2 oz. (60ml) pinot noir wine

Salty Italian sausage links are cooked sous vide with sweet bell peppers and onions, browned on the grill, and sandwiched between buns for a truly filling meal.

italian sausage
& PEPPERS

 1 hour, 45 minutes

 140°F (60°C)

 4 servings

8 Italian sausage links
2 red bell peppers, cut into strips
2 yellow bell peppers, cut into strips
1 white onion, cut into strips
1 TB. kosher salt
8 hoagie buns

PREP AND SEAL   20 minutes

1 Preheat the sous vide machine to 140°F (60°C).

2 Put Italian sausage, red bell peppers, yellow bell peppers, white onion, and kosher salt in a 1-gallon (3.75l) plastic bag or two 1-quart (1l) plastic bags and seal.

COOK   1 hour

1 Once the sous vide water bath has reached the desired temperature, insert the plastic bag of sausage and peppers and allow to cook for 1 hour.

2 Remove the plastic bag from the water bath.

FINISH   25 minutes

1 Remove Italian sausage from the plastic bag and wipe dry with paper towels. Set aside.

2 Preheat a grill on high. In a saucepan over high heat, pour peppers, onion, and juices from the plastic bag.

3 Let pepper-onion mixture simmer until there's no more liquid in the saucepan, about 8 to 10 minutes. Remove the saucepan from heat and set aside.

4 When the grill has reached the desired temperature, place Italian sausages and allow to brown for no more than 1 minute per side.

5 Divide pepper-onion mixture between hoagie buns. Place an Italian sausage link in each and serve.

PREP AND SEAL   20 minutes

1 Preheat the sous vide machine to 140°F (60°C).

2 In a small bowl, combine thyme, rosemary, black pepper, and dried orange.

3 Season pork tenderloin with dry ingredient mixture.

4 Put seasoned pork tenderloin in a 1-gallon (3.75l) plastic bag and seal.

COOK   1 hour

1 Once the sous vide water bath has reached the desired temperature, insert the plastic bag of seasoned pork tenderloin and allow to cook for 1 hour for medium-rare doneness. (See the chart in the back of the book for other doneness levels.)

2 Remove the plastic bag from the water bath.

FINISH   25 minutes

1 Remove pork tenderloin and juice from the bag, separating meat from juice.

2 Strain juice through a fine-mesh sieve into a medium bowl and set aside.

3 Dry pork tenderloin with paper towels and season with kosher salt. Coat salted pork tenderloin in vegetable oil.

4 Using a blowtorch, grill, or cast-iron skillet over high heat, sear both sides of pork tenderloin until caramelized, about 2 minutes per side. Set aside.

5 In a medium skillet over high heat, combine orange liqueur and strained juices and cook until liquid has reduced to a glaze, about 4 minutes.

6 Pour glaze over pork tenderloin. Cut glazed pork tenderloin into ⅓-inch (.75cm) slices and serve.

This delicate piece of meat is cooked sous vide for a short time to ensure it doesn't get too mushy, and then coated in an orange glaze.

orange pork
TENDERLOIN

 1 hour, 45 minutes

 140°F (60°C)

 2 servings

¼ tsp. thyme leaves

¼ tsp. rosemary leaves, chopped

½ tsp. ground black pepper

2 slices dried orange

1 (1½-lb.; 680g) whole pork tenderloin, silverskin removed

½ TB. kosher salt

1 TB. vegetable oil

¼ cup orange liqueur

Carnitas, the Mexican version of pulled pork, uses tough but flavorful pork shoulder. Cooking sous vide breaks down the connective tissue, giving you tender meat for your tacos.

carnitas

 24 hours, 45 minutes

 158°F (70°C)

 4 servings

1 white onion

4 stems fresh chopped cilantro

Juice of 1 orange

1 lb. (450g) boneless pork butt, cut into 2-in. (5cm) cubes

Peel of 1 orange

2 cloves garlic, crushed

1 bay leaf

¼ cinnamon stick, broken into 3 or 4 pieces

4 TB. lard

8 corn tortillas

1 tomatillo, husk removed and diced

1 jalapeño pepper, minced

1 cup crumbled queso fresco or feta cheese

1 lime, cut into wedges

PREP AND SEAL — 15 minutes

1 Preheat the sous vide machine to 158°F (70°C).

2 Cut white onion in half. Dice one half and, in a medium bowl, combine with cilantro and orange juice. Refrigerate until tacos are ready to serve.

3 Split remaining onion into quarters.

4 Put onion quarters, pork butt, orange peel, garlic, bay leaf, cinnamon, and lard in a 1-gallon (3.75l) plastic bag and seal.

COOK — 24 hours

1 Once the sous vide water bath has reached the desired temperature, insert the plastic bag of pork butt and seasonings and allow to cook for 24 hours.

2 Remove the plastic bag from the water bath.

FINISH — 30 minutes

1 Open a corner of the plastic bag and allow liquid to strain through a fine-mesh sieve into a medium bowl for 10 minutes.

2 Skim fat from top of liquid and add back to the plastic bag of pork butt. Remove orange peel, garlic, and spice pieces from the bag.

3 While it's still in the bag, shred pork butt by hand into pulled pork pieces. Mix well with fat that was added back.

4 Remove pork butt from the plastic bag and spread it out on a sheet pan. In an oven set to broil or using a blowtorch, sear top of carnitas until top bits are crispy, about 2 minutes.

5 Place two corn tortillas on each plate. Divide carnitas, cilantro-onion mixture, tomatillo, jalapeño, and queso fresco among tortillas. Serve plates with a lime wedge on the side.

Pork cheeks are very similar in flavor and texture to pork belly. Cooked sous vide, this lean yet moist cut becomes very tender.

SMOKED
pork cheeks

 73 hours, 10 minutes

 158°F (70°C)

 4 servings

1 TB. kosher salt
1/8 tsp. pink salt (instacure #2)
1/2 tsp. cayenne pepper
1 tsp. Hungarian paprika
1/2 tsp. ground cumin
1/2 tsp. ground black pepper
1/2 tsp. oregano
2 (1-lb.; 450g) whole pork cheeks

PREP AND SEAL   20 minutes

1 Preheat the sous vide machine to 158°F (70°C).

2 In a medium bowl, combine kosher salt, pink salt, cayenne pepper, Hungarian paprika, cumin, black pepper, and oregano.

3 Season pork cheeks with herb and spice mixture.

4 Put seasoned pork cheeks in a 1-gallon (3.75l) plastic bag and seal.

COOK   72 hours

1 Once the sous vide water bath has reached the desired temperature, insert the plastic bag of seasoned pork cheeks and allow to cook for 72 hours.

2 Remove the plastic bag from the water bath.

FINISH   50 minutes

1 Place the plastic bag into an ice bath and allow to chill for at least 20 minutes.

2 Preheat a smoker to 190°F (88°C).

3 Remove pork cheeks from the plastic bag and cut off skin. Dry pork cheeks completely with paper towels.

4 When the smoker has reached the desired temperature, place pork cheeks inside and allow to smoke for 20 minutes.

5 Remove pork cheeks from the smoker and slice into 1/4-inch (.5cm) slices.

6 Serve pork cheeks with mashed potatoes or other sides.

This Asian barbecue dish is given the sous vide treatment in this recipe. Cooking the pork belly sous vide allows the meat to stay moist during the crisping process.

CRISPY SKIN PORK
belly

 6 hours, 40 minutes

 164°F (73°C)

 4 servings

2 lb. (1kg) pork belly
2 TB. kosher salt
1 tsp. Chinese five-spice powder
1 tsp. ground black pepper
2 TB. apple cider vinegar

1 Preheat the sous vide machine to 164°F (73°C).

2 Cut through skin of pork belly at a 45-degree angle in 1-inch (2.5cm) intervals across entire belly. Cut across pork belly skin the opposite way to create perfect squares.

3 In a small bowl, combine kosher salt, Chinese five-spice powder, and black pepper. Season pork belly with dry mixture.

4 Put seasoned pork belly and apple cider vinegar in a 1-quart (1l) plastic bag and seal.

COOK   **6 hours**

1 Once the sous vide water bath has reached the desired temperature, insert the plastic bag of seasoned pork belly and allow to cook for 6 hours.

2 Remove the plastic bag from the water bath.

FINISH   **20 minutes**

1 Remove pork belly from the plastic bag and dry with paper towels.

2 Place pork belly on a rack and broil in the oven until skin is crispy, about 3 minutes.

3 Slice crispy pork belly into ¼-inch (.5cm) slices and serve.

As pork belly has increased in popularity, the cost of it has skyrocketed. If you're looking for a cheaper alternative, **pork cheeks are very similar in flavor and texture to pork belly.** If you have the opportunity, look for Berkshire breed to get the best flavor.

Smoked pork ribs are a summer grilling staple. This recipe takes the meat to new heights of flavor and moistness while allowing you to spend less time at the grill.

SMOKED PORK
ribs

 36 hours, 45 minutes

 150°F (66°C)

 4 servings

1 (4-lb.; 2kg) rack country pork ribs

2 TB. yellow mustard

3 TB. paprika

3 TB. light brown sugar, tightly packed

1 TB. oregano

1 TB. coriander

1 tsp. crushed red pepper flakes

1 tsp. pink salt (instacure #1)

1 TB. garlic powder

1 tsp. liquid smoke

½ cup barbecue sauce

PREP AND SEAL   15 minutes

1 Preheat the sous vide machine to 150°F (66°C).

2 Using a towel for grip, grab edge of silverskin on backside of pork ribs and pull off.

3 Rub both sides of rib rack with yellow mustard.

4 In a medium bowl, combine paprika, light brown sugar, oregano, coriander, crushed red pepper flakes, pink salt, and garlic powder. Sprinkle seasoning mixture on pork ribs.

5 Place seasoned pork ribs and liquid smoke in a 1-gallon (3.75l) plastic bag and seal.

COOK   36 hours

1 Once the sous vide water bath has reached the desired temperature, insert the plastic bag of seasoned pork ribs and allow to cook for 36 hours.

2 Remove the plastic bag from the water bath.

FINISH   30 minutes

1 Preheat a grill to a temperature above 600°F (316°C).

2 Remove pork ribs and from the bag and dry completely with paper towels. Set aside.

3 Strain juice from the bag through a fine-mesh sieve into a medium saucepan.

4 Add barbecue sauce to the saucepan and bring mixture to a simmer over low heat on the stovetop. Set aside.

5 Once the grill reaches the desired temperature, place pork ribs on the grill and sear for 2 minutes per side.

6 Remove pork ribs from the grill and brush with sauce. Allow to rest for 5 minutes before serving.

Fish & Shellfish

FISH & SHELLFISH
basics

Fish and shellfish may be the foods most positively influenced by the exactness of sous vide cooking. When using traditional methods, the flesh of the meat is very tender and easy to overcook, which is indicated by a white-colored film on the flesh. By dialing in the fish at the right temperature, you can retain the moisture that's typically lost during cooking.

Cooking fish and shellfish sous vide takes a bit more skill than with other proteins, as their delicate meat requires them to be handled gingerly. You must use special techniques to help them keep their shape, as well as build their texture. To aid you in this process, you'll notice many of the fish and shellfish recipes I've included in the book have a brining step.

While cooking these requires a bit more skill, don't be afraid to try out fish and shellfish sous vide. You'll be surprised how well they turn out when cooked in a way that retains the most moisture and brings out their natural flavors.

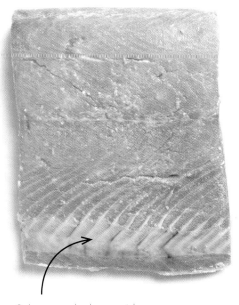

Salmon cooked sous vide

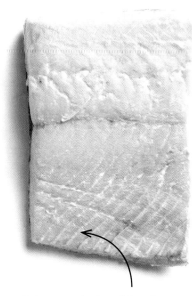

Salmon cooked traditionally

Adding a bit of **flavored oil can easily enhance the flavor of delicate fish,** as well as help it retain its shape when put into a vacuum-sealed bag. For instance, a nut oil (such as pecan or hazelnut oil) will bring a meatier flavor to salmon, while a truffle oil will give halibut a mushroom flavor.

When preparing...
Special care must be taken when vacuum sealing fish and shellfish so there's no risk of toxins. Sealing them while frozen will avoid this and help them maintain their shape while cooking. Using a zipper-lock bag and the water displacement method provides a more delicate way to work with them and lowers the possibility of foodborne illnesses.

When finishing...
Fish and shellfish may be chilled and served cold. Fish such as salmon can be put on the grill after being cooked sous vide to bring out more of its strong, smoky flavor. Scallops can be given a nice sear on the stovetop before they're combined with a light, buttery sauce. The quickest way to brown fish and seafood to bring out the umami taste is to use a blowtorch.

FISH & SHELLFISH
times & temperatures

	COOKING TEMP	TIME	SIZE/NUMBER
Blue crab	154°F (68°C)	45 minutes	8
Crab claw meat	148°F (64°C)	40 minutes	1 lb. (450g)
Lobster tails (shelled meat only)	122°F (50°C)	45 minutes	2, cut into ½-in. (1.25cm) pieces
Lump crabmeat	148°F (64°C)	40 minutes	1 lb. (450g)
Salmon fillet (cut into pieces)	125°F (52°C)	20 minutes	8 oz. (225g)
Salmon fillet (whole)	130°F (54°C)	20 minutes	½ lb. (225g), skin and pin bones removed
Scallops	122°F (50°C)	30 minutes	12 (U10 size)
Shrimp	148°F (64°C)	24 to 40 minutes	1 lb. (450g) 30-count, peeled and deveined
Tuna	122°F (50°C)	45 minutes	1 lb. (450g)

Salmon cooked sous vide

Salmon cooked traditionally

PREP AND SEAL — 10 minutes

1 Preheat the sous vide machine to 122°F (50°C).

2 Combine lobster, unsalted butter, sea salt, tarragon, chives, garlic powder, and lemon zest in a 1-quart (1l) plastic bag and seal.

COOK — 45 minutes

1 Once the sous vide water bath has reached the desired temperature, insert the plastic bag of lobster and butter sauce and allow to cook for 45 minutes.

2 Remove the plastic bag from the water bath.

FINISH — 5 minutes

1 Remove lobster from the plastic bag. Pour butter sauce into a medium bowl and set aside.

2 Place lobster pieces in toasted hot dog buns and serve with butter sauce.

To keep them from getting soggy from the lobster and sauce, you can **toast the hot dog buns in the oven.** Preheat your broiler to 500°F (260°C). Brush melted butter on the insides of the hot dog buns before placing them on a baking sheet. Allow to toast in the oven for about 1 minute, or until the inside of the buns are golden and slightly crisp.

Lobster rolls can be enjoyed cold or warm, mixed in a mayonnaise-based dressing or doused in a butter sauce. This recipe utilizes the butter sauce to perfectly cook the lobster.

LOBSTER
rolls

 1 hour

 122°F (50°C)

 2 servings

Meat from 2 lobster tails, cut into ½-in. (1.25cm) pieces
6 TB. unsalted butter, cut into pieces
1 tsp. sea salt
1 tsp. fresh tarragon, chopped
1 tsp. chives, chopped
½ tsp. garlic powder
1 tsp. lemon zest
2 hot dog buns, toasted

In this recipe, the sous vide process infuses the lime and red onion flavors directly into the naturally sweet shrimp so they are more evenly distributed across the meat.

AVOCADO SHRIMP
salad

 49 minutes

 148°F (64°C)

 4 servings

1 red onion, chopped

Juice of 2 limes

1 tsp. extra-virgin olive oil

¼ tsp. sea salt

⅛ tsp. white pepper

1 lb. (450g) raw shrimp (30 count), peeled and deveined

1 tomato, diced

1 avocado, diced

1 jalapeño, seeded and diced

1 TB. cilantro, chopped

PREP AND SEAL | 10 minutes

1 Preheat the sous vide machine to 148°F (64°C).

2 Combine red onion, lime juice, extra-virgin oil, sea salt, white pepper, and shrimp in a 1-gallon (3.75l) plastic bag and seal, making sure shrimp are in a single layer.

COOK | 24 minutes

1 Once the sous vide water bath has reached the desired temperature, insert the plastic bag of shrimp and allow to cook for 24 minutes.

2 Remove the plastic bag from the water bath.

FINISH | 15 minutes

1 Place the plastic bag in an ice bath and allow to cool for 10 minutes.

2 Meanwhile, in a large bowl, toss together tomato, avocado, jalapeño, and cilantro.

3 Top salad with cooled contents of the plastic bag and serve.

While this salad is hearty enough to be eaten by itself, **it can also be combined with other elements to make a larger meal.** Serve it wrapped in a flour tortilla or over a bed of lettuce. You can even serve the salad as an hors d'oeuvre by spooning a little of the mixture and placing the shrimp on top of slices of cucumber.

This soup of sweet coconut milk and warm spices is about as easy as it gets. You can simply put the bag in the sous vide machine and let it go.

THAI COCONUT
soup

 2 hours, 25 minutes

 153°F (67°C)

 4 servings

2 cups chicken stock

1 (15-oz.; 445ml) can unsweetened coconut milk

6 (8-oz.; 225g) bone-in chicken thighs, skin removed

2 cups shiitake mushrooms, stemmed and quartered

1 stalk fresh lemongrass, cut into 1-in. (2.5cm) pieces

1 (2-in.; 5cm) piece ginger, peeled and cut into ½-in. (1.25cm) slices

4 kaffir lime leaves

2 TB. fish sauce

4 red Thai chilies

2 tsp. granulated sugar

1 tsp. kosher salt

1 tsp. white pepper

12 sprigs fresh cilantro

1 lime, cut into wedges

1 Preheat the sous vide machine to 153°F (67°C).

2 Combine chicken stock, unsweetened coconut milk, chicken thighs, shiitake mushrooms, lemongrass, ginger, kaffir lime leaves, fish sauce, red Thai chilies, and sugar in a 1-gallon (3.75l) plastic bag and seal.

COOK   **2 hours**

1 Once the sous vide water bath has reached the desired temperature, insert the plastic bag of chicken thighs and broth and allow to cook for 2 hours.

2 Remove the plastic bag from the water bath.

FINISH   **15 minutes**

1 Remove chicken thighs from the bag, retaining broth.

2 Strain broth through a fine-mesh sieve into a large stockpot.

3 Season broth with kosher salt and white pepper. Bring to a simmer over high heat for 5 minutes. Remove from heat and set aside.

4 Debone chicken and chop meat into small pieces. Divide chicken pieces among serving bowls.

5 Pour the hot broth over chicken pieces in the bowls and serve each with 3 sprigs cilantro and 1 lime wedge.

This spread combines the smoky taste of salmon with a creamy and refreshing lemon-butter sauce for a decadent appetizer.

SALMON
rillettes

 2 hours, 40 minutes

 130°F (54°C)

 8 servings

1 (½-lb.; 225g) salmon fillet, skin and pin bones removed

1 tsp. sea salt

6 TB. unsalted butter

2 shallots, peeled and minced

1 garlic clove, peeled and minced

½ oz. (15ml) lemon juice

PREP AND SEAL   10 minutes

1 Preheat the sous vide machine to 130°F (54°C).

2 Combine salmon fillet, sea salt, unsalted butter, shallots, garlic clove, and lemon juice in a 1-quart (1l) plastic bag and seal.

COOK   20 minutes

1 Once the sous vide water bath has reached the desired temperature, insert the plastic bag of salmon and lemon-butter sauce and allow to cook for 20 minutes.

2 Remove the plastic bag from the water bath.

FINISH   2 hours, 10 minutes

1 With the bag still sealed, break up salmon fillet into small pieces.

2 Divide salmon pieces among eight crocks. Top each crock with lemon-butter sauce from the bag.

3 Place the crocks in the refrigerator and allow to chill for at least 2 hours.

4 Serve as a spread with crusty slices of bread.

Rillettes is a preservation technique that once allowed people to keep their salmon for months. While refrigeration is readily available now, the food is good enough that people crave it for its flavor still. Using sous vide to perform the technique results in a fresher and more flavorful product.

PREP AND SEAL   10 minutes

1 Preheat the sous vide machine to 183°F (84°C).

2 In a medium bowl, mix kosher salt and cold water until salt dissolves; this forms a brine.

3 In a zipper-lock bag, place salmon fillet pieces and brine. Seal the bag and put in a refrigerator for 1 hour.

4 Meanwhile, place beets, orange juice, and honey in a 1-gallon (3.75l) plastic bag and seal.

COOK   1 hour, 20 minutes

1 Once the sous vide water bath has reached the desired temperature, insert the plastic bag of beets and allow to cook for 1 hour.

2 Remove the plastic bag from the water bath and hold at room temperature.

3 Add a few ice cubes to the water bath to bring the temperature down to 125°F (52°C).

4 Remove salmon pieces from brine and rinse under cold water. Place salmon pieces in a 1-quart (1l) plastic bag and seal.

5 Once the sous vide water bath has reached the desired temperature, insert the plastic bag of salmon pieces and allow to cook for 20 minutes.

6 Remove the plastic bag from the water bath.

FINISH   20 minutes

1 Preheat a grill to a temperature above 600°F (316°C).

2 Remove salmon pieces from the bag, dry completely with paper towels, and coat with vegetable oil.

3 Once the grill reaches the desired temperature, place salmon pieces on the grill and cook for 1 minute on each side. Remove salmon pieces from the grill and set aside.

4 Divide frisée lettuce between bowls and top lettuce with beet pieces. Garnish each with 8 mandarin orange pieces, 2 ounces (55g) blue cheese, and 16 pecans.

5 Top each beet salad with 2 pieces grilled salmon and serve.

Salmon is brined and then cooked–ensuring an end product that's not mushy–before being placed on top of a refreshing beet salad for an explosion of taste.

grilled salmon
& BEET SALAD

 1 hour, 50 minutes

 183°F (84°C) and 125°F (52°C)

 2 servings

¼ cup kosher salt

1 qt. (1l) cold water

1 (8-oz.; 225g) salmon fillet, cut into 4 pieces

4 beets, peeled and cut into ½-in. (1.25cm) pieces

¼ cup orange juice

2 TB. honey

2 TB. vegetable oil

1 head frisée lettuce, root end removed

16 mandarin orange pieces

4 oz. (110g) blue cheese, crumbled

32 pecans, toasted

Brining the tuna and then cooking it sous vide with oil and lemon zest yields fish with a bright flavor and firm texture that can be enjoyed atop pastas or salads.

TUNA
confit

 1 hour, 55 minutes

 122°F (50°C)

 4 servings

2 cups water
1 TB. kosher salt
1 TB. granulated sugar
1 lb. (450g) fresh tuna
2 TB. extra-virgin olive oil
1 tsp. lemon zest

PREP AND SEAL   45 minutes

1 Preheat the sous vide machine to 122°F (50°C).

2 In a medium bowl, mix water, kosher salt, and sugar until salt and sugar dissolve; this forms a brine.

3 In a zipper-lock bag, place tuna and brine. Seal the bag and put in a refrigerator for 30 minutes.

4 Remove tuna from the bag and dry completely with paper towels.

5 Combine tuna, extra-virgin olive oil, and lemon zest in a 1-quart (1l) plastic bag and seal.

COOK   45 minutes

1 Once the sous vide water bath has reached the desired temperature, insert the plastic bag of tuna and allow to cook for 45 minutes.

2 Remove the plastic bag from the water bath.

FINISH   25 minutes

1 Remove tuna from the bag, discarding other ingredients.

2 Chill tuna in an ice bath for 20 minutes before storing, or serve hot immediately.

The nice thing about this recipe is once this tuna is cooked, **it can be stored for several days until used.** This is a great way to cook fish that you know you won't be able to eat right away.

Creating the roux via the stovetop and oven while cooking the seafood and vegetables sous vide allows you to put together a gumbo for guests that's short on time and long on flavor.

SEAFOOD
gumbo

 1 hour, 45 minutes

 148°F (64°C)

 12 servings

1 cup all-purpose flour

1½ cups vegetable oil

3 qt. (3l) seafood stock

1 lb. (450g) raw shrimp (30 count), peeled and deveined

1 lb. (450g) lump crabmeat

1 lb. (450g) crab claw meat

1 white onion, diced

2 stalks celery, diced

1 green bell pepper, diced

24 shucked oysters, liquid reserved

Kosher salt

Ground black pepper

Cayenne pepper

2 tsp. filé powder

2 cups steamed white rice

1 cup green onions, chopped

PREP AND SEAL — 45 minutes

1 Preheat the sous vide machine to 148°F (64°C) and an oven to 250°F (121°C).

2 In a medium iron skillet heated to medium, add all-purpose flour and vegetable oil. Whisk until roux smells nutty, about 3 minutes.

3 Once the oven has reached the desired temperature, insert skillet of roux and allow to cook for 40 minutes, whisking occasionally to prevent it from burning.

4 Meanwhile, divide seafood stock, shrimp, lump crabmeat, crab claw meat, white onion, celery, and green bell pepper between two 1-gallon (3.75l) plastic bags and seal.

COOK — 40 minutes

1 Once the sous vide water bath has reached the desired temperature, insert the plastic bag of seafood and vegetables and allow to cook for 40 minutes.

2 Remove the plastic bag from the water bath.

FINISH — 20 minutes

1 Pour roux into a large stockpot, place on the stovetop over medium heat, and allow to come to a simmer. Pour in reserved oyster liquid and broth from the bags and whisk until combined.

2 Reduce heat to medium-low and allow to cook for 10 minutes. Add solids from the bags and stir in until just incorporated.

3 Season gumbo to taste with kosher salt, black pepper, and cayenne pepper. Add filé powder to thicken slightly.

4 Divide white rice among bowls. Top each with gumbo, 2 oysters, and a sprinkle of green onions and serve.

This recipe uses sous vide technology to cook the crab until tender and juicy, to emulsify a hollandaise, and to poach eggs, making a typically complicated process much easier.

crab
EGGS BENEDICT

🕐 2 hours, 30 minutes

🔥 154°F (68°C) and 167°F (75°C)

🍴 4 servings

Crab Cakes:
8 blue crabs
⅓ cup crushed butter crackers
1 green onion (green and white parts), finely chopped
½ cup red bell pepper, diced small
¼ cup mayonnaise
1 large egg
1 tsp. Worcestershire sauce
1 tsp. dry mustard
Juice of ½ lemon
¼ tsp. garlic powder
1 tsp. sea salt
½ cup peanut oil
¼ cup all-purpose flour

Hollandaise:
1½ oz. (15ml) champagne vinegar
½ shallot, minced
10 TB. butter
2 large egg yolks
¼ cup water
Juice of ½ lemon
¼ tsp. kosher salt

Poached Eggs:
4 large eggs

Assembly:
2 English muffins, toasted

1 Preheat the sous vide machine to 154°F (68°C).

2 Bring a large stockpot halfway filled with water to a boil. Place blue crabs in boiling water, cover, and allow to boil for 1 minute. Remove blue crabs to an ice bath and allow to cool for 1 minute.

3 Remove legs from body of blue crabs. Package both legs and bodies in a 1-quart (1l) plastic bag and seal.

COOK 2 hours

1 Once the sous vide water bath has reached the desired temperature, insert the plastic bag of blue crabs and allow to cook for 45 minutes.

2 Remove the plastic bag from the water bath. Place the bag in an ice bath and allow to cool for 10 minutes.

3 Raise the temperature of the sous vide bath to 167°F (75°C).

4 Pick meat from cooled blue crab shells.

5 In a large bowl, combine butter cracker crumbs, green onion, green bell pepper, mayonnaise, egg, Worcestershire sauce, dry mustard, lemon juice, garlic powder, and sea salt. Fold pieces of blue crab into mixture.

6 Divide mixture into four crab cakes. Place in the freezer and allow to chill for 15 minutes.

7 In a medium cast-iron skillet over high heat, preheat peanut oil. Dust both sides of crab cakes with all-purpose flour. Add crab cakes to the skillet and quickly fry on each side until golden brown, taking care not to overcook, about 45 seconds. Set aside.

8 In a medium sauté pan over high heat, combine champagne vinegar and shallots and allow to cook until volume of vinegar is reduced by half. Strain vinegar reduction, saving liquid and discarding solids.

9 Combine vinegar reduction, butter, egg yolks, water, lemon juice, and kosher salt in a 1-quart (1l) plastic bag and seal.

10 Once the sous vide water bath has reached the desired temperature, insert the plastic bag of hollandaise and allow to cook for 30 minutes.

11 Remove the plastic bag from the water bath. Pour hollandaise sauce into a siphon whip dispenser and charge with two N_2O canisters. Hold in the sous vide bath until ready for use.

12 Place eggs in shell in the sous vide bath still set to 167°F (75°C) for 13 minutes.

FINISH 15 minutes

1 Place ½ of toasted English muffin on each plate. Place crab cake on each muffin half.

2 Break each poached egg into a small bowl. Using a slotted spoon, place egg on top of crab cake.

3 Top each crab cake with whipped hollandaise and serve.

These scallops are cooked sous vide with lemon and honey before searing, and then coated in an orange-flavored beurre blanc (white butter) sauce for a dish that's light and refreshing.

The key to a good sear on scallops is to **make sure they're packed without chemicals** when they're shipped to the grocery store—a process known as *dry packing.* Look for this label or ask a seafood monger to direct you to the correct packaging of scallops.

LEMON-SEARED
scallops

 1 hour, 10 minutes

 122°F (50°C)

 4 servings

12 dry-packed scallops (U10 size)
1 lemon, sliced into rings
1 TB. honey
1 TB. kosher salt
1 tsp. white pepper
1 oz. (25ml) vegetable oil
2 oz. (60ml) dry sherry
1 TB. orange juice
4 TB. very cold whole butter, cut into small pieces

PREP AND SEAL   10 minutes

1 Preheat the sous vide machine to 122°F (50°C).

2 Place dry-packed scallops in a single layer in a 1-quart (1l) plastic bag. Top with lemon and honey and seal.

COOK   30 minutes

1 Once the sous vide water bath has reached the desired temperature, insert the plastic bag of scallops and allow to cook for 30 minutes.

2 Remove the plastic bag from the water bath.

FINISH   30 minutes

1 Remove scallops from the bag, reserving honey and lemon in the bag.

2 Dry scallops with paper towels and season with kosher salt and white pepper.

3 Preheat vegetable oil in a medium cast-iron skillet over high heat until it's smoking. Add scallops and sear both sides for about 45 seconds per side. Remove from the skillet and set aside.

4 Add dry sherry to the still-hot skillet and let simmer over high heat until sherry has reduced to the point it's almost gone, about 45 seconds.

5 Reduce heat to medium. Add honey and lemon from the bag and orange juice to the skillet, and bring to a simmer. Immediately remove the skillet from the stovetop.

6 Whisk whole butter into the skillet to make beurre blanc sauce.

7 Serve scallops coated in beurre blanc sauce.

Desserts

DESSERT
basics

Traditionally, when baking cakes, pies, and cookies, there's a big jump in the volume of the batter that happens right when you put it in the preheated oven (known as *oven spring*). This is duplicated in sous vide by **preheating the bath to 195°F (91°C)** before putting the dessert in it

Desserts cooked sous vide? Many people often question how it's possible to make dessert–even ice cream–using the sous vide process. In reality, baking is considered much more of a science than cooking savory foods, so when it comes to the science of exact heat, bakers tend to grasp the concept of sous vide very quickly.

The difference you'll find from traditional baking in terms of the end result is astounding. Cookies are chewier (with less butter!), cakes have a delicate crumb, pies are richer, and cobblers are airier when cooked sous vide.

Another big difference you'll find is what the dessert is cooked in. Baking dessert automatically calls to mind precise containers, such as a 9×13-inch (23×33cm) cake pan. However, many of these don't work with a sous vide water bath due to size restrictions. Instead, we go back to a sous vide tradition–glass jars. So when you cook a cake in a glass jar, for instance, not only will you get a delicious dessert, you'll have a more modern presentation that really wows your guests.

When preparing...

Make sure you use a nonstick cooking spray to keep the baked good from sticking when using jars. Also, when you put the jars into the sous vide bath, don't be too concerned about whether the water level goes over the top. The water simply needs to be high enough to go above the volume of the batter.

When finishing...

Desserts may be finished by chilling them, topping them with berries, or frosting them. If you're using frosting, you have the option of making the frosting sous vide and then pouring it into a siphon whipping dispenser. You can then charge the dispenser with two N_2O canisters before spraying the frosting on the dessert.

Sponge cake cooked sous vide

DESSERT
times & temperatures

	COOKING TEMP	TIME	SIZE/NUMBER
Berry consommé	190°F (88°C)	45 minutes	2 cups
Chocolate chip cookies	195°F (91°C)	3 hours	24 cookies
Peach cobbler	195°F (91°C)	3 hours	6 half-pint-size (235ml) jars
Pecan pie	195°F (91°C)	2 hours	8 pint-size (470ml) jars
Sponge cake	195°F (91°C)	3 hours	8 pint-size (470ml) jars
Vanilla ice cream	185°F (85°C)	1 hour	6 cups
White chocolate cheesecake	176°F (80°C)	2 hours	8 pint-size (470ml) jars

Sponge cake cooked traditionally

PREP AND SEAL   5 minutes

1 Preheat the sous vide machine to 190°F (88°C).

2 Combine frozen berries and sugar in a 1-quart (1l) plastic bag and seal.

COOK   45 minutes

1 Once the sous vide water bath has reached the desired temperature, insert the plastic bag of sugared berries and allow to cook for 45 minutes.

2 Remove the plastic bag from the water bath.

FINISH   10 minutes

1 Open the bag and pour berries and juice into a large serving bowl, or spoon out of the bag into four individual portions.

2 Serve consommé as a sauce on ice creams or panna cotta, or even as a soup.

Consommé prepared sous vide yields a juice that's clear and bright in flavor. Experiment with your favorite berries and taste for yourself!

berry
CONSOMMÉ

 1 hour

 190°F (88°C)

 4 servings

2 lb. (1kg) frozen berries
¼ cup granulated sugar

The sous vide method for consommé **works best when using frozen berries.** This is because the cell walls of the frozen versions are brittle, so when the fruit is cooked, you'll get more juice.

These little cakes–baked in sealed jars–have a moist texture and a delicate crumb. They're finished off with a decadent sous vide chocolate frosting.

sponge cake

 4 hours, 20 minutes

 195°F (91°C) and 142°F (61°C)

 8 servings

Cake:
2 cups cake flour
1 tsp. baking powder
½ tsp. kosher salt
1 stick unsalted butter, at room temperature
1 cup granulated sugar
2 large eggs, at room temperature
1 tsp. vanilla extract
1 cup buttermilk, at room temperature

Frosting:
4 TB. butter
3 TB. cocoa powder
¼ cup whole milk
1 tsp. vanilla extract
2½ cups powdered sugar

PREP AND SEAL   30 minutes

1 Preheat the sous vide machine to 195°F (91°C).

2 Spray the inside of eight individual pint-size (470ml) glass canning jars with nonstick cooking spray.

3 Sift together cake flour, baking powder, and kosher salt into a medium bowl. Set aside.

4 In a second medium bowl, while using an electric mixer with a paddle attachment, combine unsalted butter and sugar on a medium setting for 7 minutes. Mixture should become light and airy.

5 With the mixer still running on medium, add eggs one at a time to butter-sugar mixture, allowing egg to be incorporated before adding next one. Add vanilla extract and mix until combined.

6 Turn down the mixer to a low setting and add sifted ingredients a little at a time. Mix until incorporated.

7 With the mixer still running on low, add buttermilk and mix until all ingredients are combined.

8 Divide cake batter among the jars and seal with the lids.

COOK   3 hours, 30 minutes

1 Once the sous vide water bath has reached the desired temperature, insert the jars of batter, making sure they sit flat on the bottom of the bath. (The jars don't have to be fully covered with water.) Allow to cook for 3 hours. Remove the jars from the water bath.

2 Reduce the temperature of the sous vide machine to 142°F (61°C).

3 Place butter, cocoa powder, whole milk, vanilla extract, and powdered sugar in a 1-quart (1l) plastic bag and seal. Shake the bag to mix ingredients.

4 Once the sous vide water bath has reached the desired temperature, insert the plastic bag of frosting and allow to cook for 30 minutes. Remove the plastic bag from the water bath.

FINISH   20 minutes

1 Pour frosting into a siphon whipping dispenser and charge with two N$_2$O canisters.

2 Spray frosting on cakes in the jars and serve, or pop cakes out of the jars, spray on frosting, and serve.

Baking cookies sous vide requires a lower concentration of butter so they'll rise. But don't worry—they'll be even more delicious than ones right from the oven.

CHOCOLATE CHIP
cookies

 3 hours, 50 minutes

 195°F (91°C)

 12 to 24 servings

6 TB. unsalted butter, at room temperature

⅓ cup dark brown sugar, tightly packed

⅓ cup light brown sugar, tightly packed

1 large egg

¼ tsp. salt

1 cup all-purpose flour

2 tsp. vanilla extract

1 tsp. baking powder

1 cup semisweet chocolate chips

PREP AND SEAL — 30 minutes

1 Preheat the sous vide machine to 195°F (91°C).

2 Spray the inside of two 1-quart (1l) plastic bags with nonstick cooking spray.

3 In a large bowl, while using an electric mixer with a paddle attachment, beat unsalted butter, dark brown sugar, and light brown sugar on a high setting until mixture looks like heavy cream, about 5 minutes.

4 Add egg and beat for 3 minutes. Add salt and all-purpose flour and beat for 2 minutes.

5 Add vanilla extract and baking powder and mix on a medium setting for 1 minute.

6 Add semisweet chocolate chips and mix on a low setting just enough to incorporate into dough.

7 Divide dough in two and place each half in a prepared plastic bag.

8 Roll a rolling pin over the bags to diminish dough thickness to ¼ inch (.5cm) and seal.

COOK — 3 hours

1 Once the sous vide water bath has reached the desired temperature, insert the plastic bags of dough and allow to cook for 3 hours.

2 Remove the plastic bags from the water bath.

FINISH — 20 minutes

1 Allow the bags to rest for 10 minutes before opening.

2 Cut the plastic bags off of whole cookie.

3 Cut cookie into 24 2-inch (5cm) circles and serve.

Traditionally a baked dessert consisting of biscuits atop stewed peaches, peach cobbler cooked sous vide allows the peaches to retain a brighter flavor, with the biscuit rising as it cooks.

PEACH
cobbler

 3 hours, 30 minutes

 195°F (91°C)

6 servings

3 cups peeled and diced freestone peaches (2 to 3 medium)
8 TB. unsalted butter, at room temperature
1 cup granulated sugar
1 tsp. vanilla extract
1 tsp. almond extract
1 cup whole milk
1 cup self-rising flour

PREP AND SEAL   20 minutes

1 Preheat the sous vide machine to 195°F (91°C).

2 Spray the inside of six individual half-pint-size (235ml) glass canning jars with nonstick cooking spray. Divide freestone peaches evenly among the jars.

3 In a medium bowl, while using an electric mixer with a paddle attachment, combine unsalted butter and sugar on a medium setting for 5 minutes.

4 Reduce the mixer speed to low. Add vanilla extract, almond extract, and whole milk and mix until fully incorporated.

5 Add self-rising flour and mix until incorporated. Some lumps are good—don't overmix.

6 Pour batter evenly among the jars and seal with the lids.

COOK   3 hours

1 Once the sous vide water bath has reached the desired temperature, insert the jars of batter and allow to cook for 3 hours.

2 Remove the jars from the water bath.

FINISH   10 minutes

1 Remove the lids and finish by browning top of each cobbler with a blowtorch.

2 Serve cobbler in the jars while still warm.

Sous vide cooks this cheesecake at a high-enough temperature to fully incorporate the white chocolate and allow the eggs to cook while still keeping the batter light and airy.

WHITE CHOCOLATE
cheese cake

 6 hours, 35 minutes

 176°F (80°C)

 8 servings

16 oz. (450g) cream cheese, softened to room temperature

¼ cup sour cream

2 TB. granulated sugar

3 large eggs

1 tsp. cake flour

1 tsp. vanilla extract

10 oz. (285g) white chocolate

PREP AND SEAL   **30 minutes**

1 Preheat the sous vide machine to 176°F (80°C).

2 In a medium bowl, while using an electric mixer with a paddle attachment, combine cream cheese, sour cream, and sugar on a medium setting until fully incorporated.

3 With the mixer still running on medium, add eggs one at a time, allowing egg to be incorporated before adding next one. Add cake flour and vanilla extract and mix for 3 seconds. Set aside.

4 In a small microwave-safe bowl, put white chocolate. Place the bowl in the microwave and heat on high in 30-second intervals, mixing in between, until chocolate is melted.

5 Add melted chocolate to cheesecake batter and use a spatula to combine.

6 Divide batter among eight individual pint-size (470ml) glass canning jars and seal with the lids.

COOK   **2 hours**

1 Once the sous vide water bath has reached the desired temperature, insert the jars of batter (making sure they rest flat on the bottom) and allow to cook for 2 hours.

2 Remove the jars from the water bath.

FINISH   **4 hours, 5 minutes**

1 Place the jars in the refrigerator and allow to chill for 4 hours.

2 Serve as is or topped with seasonal fruit.

1 Preheat the sous vide machine to 195°F (91°C).

2 In a medium bowl, whisk together maple syrup, light brown sugar, heavy whipping cream, molasses, kosher salt, vanilla extract, bourbon whiskey, and egg yolks.

3 In a small microwave-safe bowl, melt unsalted butter. Add melted butter to the medium bowl and whisk.

4 Divide mixture among eight individual pint-size (470ml) glass canning jars, top each with ¼ cup pecans, and seal with the lids.

COOK   2 hours

1 Once the sous vide water bath has reached the desired temperature, insert the jars of batter and allow to cook for 2 hours.

2 Remove the jars from the water bath.

FINISH   4 hours, 5 minutes

1 Place the jars on a cooling rack and allow to cool for 4 hours.

2 Serve in the jars with a dollop of whipped cream.

It's very easy to make **whipped cream from scratch.** Start by chilling a large bowl and the tool you plan to use (whether it's a whisk or a whisk attachment) for 20 minutes. When ready, add 1 cup cold heavy whipping cream, 2 tablespoons granulated sugar, and ½ teaspoon sugar in the bowl and whisk by hand or using a mixer with a whisk attachment on high for 1 minute, or until stiff peaks form.

A well-made pecan pie has a sweet taste and a nutty crunch. The sous vide process helps lock in the mouth-watering smells of molasses and bourbon in this crustless version.

pecan
PIE

 6 hours, 25 minutes

 195°F (91°C)

8 servings

1 cup real maple syrup

1 cup light brown sugar, tightly packed

½ cup heavy whipping cream

1 TB. molasses

½ tsp. kosher salt

1 tsp. vanilla extract

1 TB. bourbon whiskey

7 large egg yolks

4 TB. unsalted butter

2 cups whole pecans, toasted

Store-bought or freshly whipped cream

This simple and time-honored treat gets the sous vide treatment. Top with nuts or crumbled cookies to create a taste sensation.

vanilla
ICE CREAM

 2 hours, 40 minutes

 185°F (85°C)

 6 servings

2¼ cups milk
2¼ cups heavy cream
5 large egg yolks
1 cup granulated sugar
1 tsp. vanilla extract

1 Preheat the sous vide machine to 185°F (85°C).

2 Combine milk, heavy cream, egg yolks, sugar, and vanilla extract in a 1-gallon (3.75l) plastic bag and seal.

3 Shake the bag until sugar has dissolved and egg yolks are incorporated.

1 Once the sous vide water bath has reached the desired temperature, insert the plastic bag of ice cream mixture and allow to cook for 1 hour, removing and shaking the bag every 15 minutes.

2 Remove the plastic bag from the water bath.

1 Place the plastic bag in an ice bath and allow to completely cool, about 1 hour.

2 Pour chilled mixture into an ice cream maker and freeze according to the manufacturer's directions.

3 Serve immediately or store in the freezer for up to 2 months.

Making ice cream sous vide eliminates the stovetop process typically used for the base. This allows you to **capture the smooth texture you desire without worrying about the eggs curdling** during cooking.

SOUS VIDE COOKING
times & temperatures

Type	Cooking Temp	Time
FRUITS & VEGETABLES		
Apples	185°F (85°C)	1 hour
Artichokes	182°F (83°C)	30 minutes
Asparagus	190°F (88°C)	4 minutes
Baby beets	182°F (83°C)	1 hour
Baby carrots	185°F (85°C)	1 hour, 15 minutes
Cauliflower	183°F (84°C)	2 hours
Corn	185°F (85°C)	2 hours
Fennel	185°F (85°C)	1 hour
Kidney beans	190°F (88°C)	6 hours
Leeks	185°F (85°C)	20 minutes
Navy beans	190°F (88°C)	6 hours
Pearl onions	185°F (85°C)	1 hour, 30 minutes
Pickled beets	190°F (88°C)	40 minutes
Radishes	182°F (83°C)	45 minutes
Red cabbage	183°F (84°C)	45 minutes
Red potatoes	190°F (88°C)	1 hour
Russet potatoes	190°F (88°C)	1 hour
	194°F (90°C)	25 minutes
Shiitake mushrooms	185°F (85°C)	dried: 45 minutes; fresh: 20 minutes

Type	Cooking Temp	Time
Sweet potatoes	185°F (85°C)	1 hour
Turnips	185°F (85°C)	2 hours

POULTRY

Type	Cooking Temp	Time
Chicken breasts (diced)	147°F (64°C)	1 hour
Chicken breasts (whole)	145°F (63°C), 147°F (64°C), or 150°F (66°C)	1 hour
Chicken thighs (bone in)	147°F (64°C)	1 hour, 30 minutes
	154°F (68°C)	1 hour
Chicken thighs (boneless)	154°F (68°C)	6 hours
Chicken wings	150°F (66°C)	2 hours
Duck legs	170°F (77°C)	12 hours
Eggs	poached: 145°F (63°C); soft-boiled: 150°F (66°C); hard-boiled: 165°F (74°C)	1 hour
Turkey breasts	145°F (63°C)	4 hours
Whole chicken (cooked in 1 bag)	147°F (64°C)	3 hours
Whole chicken (cooked in 2 bags)	thighs and legs (dark meat): 155°F (68°C) and 145°F (63°C)	2 hours
	breast halves and wings (white meat): 145°F (63°C)	1 hour
Whole chicken (cut into quarters)	147°F (64°C)	1 hour, 30 minutes

BEEF & LAMB

Type	Cooking Temp	Time
Beef brisket	153°F (67°C)	36 hours
	180°F (82°C)	10 hours
Beef chuck roast	179°F (82°C)	8 hours
Beef flank	134°F (57°C)	6 hours

Type	Cooking Temp	Time
Beef knuckle	135°F (57°C)	48 hours
Beef shank	131°F (55°C)	48 hours
Beef spare ribs	130°F (54°C)	72 hours
	140°F (60°C)	48 hours
Beef stew meat	149°F (65°C) to 150°F (66°C)	16 hours
Ground beef	rare: 127°F (53°C); medium rare: 135°F (57°C); medium: 145°F (63°C); medium well: 150°F (66°C); well: 155°F (68°C)	1 hour
Lamb shoulder	133°F (56°C)	3 hours
	149°F (65°C)	16 hours
Rack of lamb	129°F (54°C)	1 hour
Rib-eye	rare: 127°F (53°C); medium rare: 133°F (56°C); medium: 145°F (63°C); medium well: 150°F (66°C); well: 155°F (68°C)	1 hour
Veal loin chop	140°F (60°C)	30 minutes
PORK		
Country pork ribs	150°F (66°C)	36 hours
Ground pork	150°F (66°C)	1 hour
Ham hock	132°F (56°C)	72 hours
Italian sausage	140°F (60°C)	1 hour
Pork belly	164°F (73°C)	6 hours
Pork butt	158°F (70°C)	24 hours
Pork chops	rare: 125°F (52°C); medium rare: 140°F (60°C); medium: 145°F (63°C); medium well: 150°F (66°C); well: 155°F (68°C)	45 minutes to 1 hour

Type	Cooking Temp	Time
Pork roast	136°F (58°C)	5 hours
Whole pork cheeks	158°F (70°C)	72 hours
Whole tenderloin	rare: 125°F (52°C); medium rare: 140°F (60°C); medium: 145°F (63°C); medium well: 150°F (66°C); well: 155°F (68°C)	45 minutes to 1 hour

FISH & SHELLFISH

Type	Cooking Temp	Time
Blue crab	154°F (68°C)	45 minutes
Crab claw meat	148°F (64°C)	40 minutes
Lobster tails (shelled meat only)	122°F (50°C)	45 minutes
Lump crabmeat	148°F (64°C)	40 minutes
Salmon fillet (cut into pieces)	125°F (52°C)	20 minutes
Salmon fillet (whole)	130°F (54°C)	20 minutes
Scallops	122°F (50°C)	30 minutes
Shrimp	148°F (64°C)	24 to 40 minutes
Tuna	122°F (50°C)	45 minutes

DESSERTS

Type	Cooking Temp	Time
Berry consommé	190°F (88°C)	45 minutes
Chocolate chip cookies	195°F (91°C)	3 hours
Peach cobbler	195°F (91°C)	3 hours
Pecan pie	195°F (91°C)	2 hours
Sponge cake	195°F (91°C)	3 hours
Vanilla ice cream	185°F (85°C)	1 hour
White chocolate cheesecake	176°F (80°C)	2 hours

index

R–S

T

About the Author

Chef Thomas N. England is a professional chef, food writer, educator, and mentor who has shared his expertise with many aspiring and seasoned chefs for over 20 years. Born and raised in northern Indiana, Chef England trained in New York at the Culinary Institute of America. He spent much of his professional career in New York, as well as in central Indiana. He is an ACF-certified executive chef (CEC) and a certified food service educator (CFSE). As a certified specialist of spirits (CSS), he is also well versed in the production and pairing of alcohol, running and consulting for wineries.

Chef England currently serves as program coordinator at the Ivy Tech Hospitality and Culinary Arts program. Additionally, he is active in the community as a local foods activist as co-founder and president of Dig-IN, a nonprofit for the promotion of Indiana Food, Beverage, and Agriculture.

He is the author of three cookbooks, including *Idiots Guides: Grilling, Idiots Guides: Cooking Basics,* and *Indiana Harvest.* Over the years, Chef England has also had food articles published in several local and national publications. He has been an avid local foods traveler, studying food and culture in 47 states and 7 countries.

Acknowledgments

There are several people I would like to thank. Without their guidance and support, it would not have been possible for me to write this book.

A huge thank-you to the faculty and students at Ivy Tech Community College of Central Indiana. Working with thousands of Ivy Tech students over the past 10 years has filled my life with memories and life lessons. It is the support of the college that allows me the professional development to research emerging techniques and gives me the encouragement to write.

The team of people making sure that every picture had the right details was amazing. Students Nina Baker, Chante Cramp, Paul Fesenmeier, Regina Huston, Jordan Smith, and Laresa Smith—led by Trisha LeBlanc—cooked the foods. It was then perfectly styled and shot by a team of five others.

Writing is truly a team effort. A huge thank-you to the team at Alpha Books that make these words seem effortless. The teams of editors who have scoured the book and the artistic people that make it look good are the people that really make this book happen. Special thanks to Kayla Dugger for making sure the details are taken care of.

My mother and brother, Joanna and Tony England, are the reason I followed my passion for food and drink. They have always encouraged me to follow my nose. Thank you for all that you do to lead when I need direction—and for listening when I talk incessantly about food and drink details.